Changing the School Learning Environment

Where Do We Stand after Decades of Reform?

Edited by
Jack Frymier
Ronald G. Joekel

ScarecrowEducation
Lanham, Maryland • Toronto • Oxford
2004

Published in the United States of America
by ScarecrowEducation
An imprint of The Rowman & Littlefield Publishing Group, Inc.
4501 Forbes Boulevard, Suite 200, Lanham, Maryland 20706
www.scarecroweducation.com

PO Box 317
Oxford
OX2 9RU, UK

British Library Cataloguing in Publication Information Available

Library of Congress Cataloging-in-Publication Data

Changing the school learning environment : where do we stand after decades
of reform? / edited by Jack Frymier, Ronald G. Joekel.
    p. cm.
  Includes bibliographical references and index.
  ISBN 1-57886-118-7 (pbk. : alk. paper)
  1. Education, Secondary—United States—Evaluation. 2. School improvement programs—United States—Evaluation. 3. Public schools—United
States—Evaluation. I. Frymier, Jack Rimmel, 1925– II. Joekel, Ronald.

LA222.C445 2004
373.2'5'0973—dc22

                                                                    2004000059

This book is dedicated by the members of the Learning Environments Consortium International Forum to Dr. William Den Hertog Georgiades. Bill Georgiades began a long and distinguished career in education as a high school teacher and administrator in Southern California. He moved to higher education first as professor and associate dean of education at the University of Southern California (1956–1979) and then as dean and professor of education at the University of Houston (1979–1994). He concluded his higher education career as executive director of international education at the University of Houston (1994–1998). He was a Fulbright scholar and lecturer in Cyprus and Greece. He served as associate director of the Model Schools Project supported by the National Association of Secondary School Principals and the Danforth Foundation (1968–1977) and was the founding president of the Learning Environments Consortium International, which he served from 1975 until his death in 2001.

Bill Georgiades embodied what many think of as quintessential American virtues: a democratic outlook, a religious spirit, a way with words, the capacity to see an important goal and pursue it, real generosity to both friends and rivals, and grace under pressure. He made a significant impact on education in the United States, Canada, Europe, and the Near East. He inspired and guided his family, friends, and colleagues and countless others in his personal and professional life. He leaves behind his influence, his body of work, and a legacy of commitment to educational renewal that will never entirely be forgotten.

Contents

List of Abbreviations

IDEA	Institute for Development of Educational Activities
CASE-IMS	Comprehensive Assessment of School Environments Information Management System
CBE	Competency-Based Education
CCSDL	Canadian Coalition for Self-Directed Learning
CES	Coalition of Essential Schools
CIPP	context-input-process product
CORE	Curriculum Objective Referenced Evaluation
CORS	Center on Organization and Restructuring of Schools
CPE	Central Park East Secondary School
CPM	Critical Path Method
CSRD	Comprehensive School Reform Demonstration
DPIE	diagnosis, prescription, implementation, and evaluation
IGE	Individually Guided Education
IP	in progress
IPP	Individualized Personal Plan
IS	independent study
LEAD	Leadership in Educational Administration Development
LEC	Learning Environments Consortium
LECI	Learning Environments Consortium International
LG	large group
LGP	large group presentations
MBO	Management by Objective
MSP	Model Schools Project
NAS	New American Schools

NASA	National Aeronautics and Space Administration
NASSP	National Association of Secondary School Principals
NCLB	No Child Left Behind
OD	organizational development
OR	Operations Research
PERT	Program Evaluation and Review Technique
PPBES	Planning, Programming, Budgeting, and Evaluation Systems
SG	small group
SGD	small group discussion
SLT	School Leadership Team
SM/DT	School Management/Design Team
SMT	Supervisory Management Team
STAD	Student Teams-Achievement Division
TA	teaching assistant
TGT	teams, games, and tournaments
WCER	Wisconsin Center for Education Research

Introduction: A New Education for a New World

James W. Keefe

In 1962, President John F. Kennedy reflected on the astounding scientific progress of the twentieth century. He wanted to provide an understandable perspective of the space age so he set forth a fanciful scenario to illustrate the enormity of the changes mankind has seen. He suggested that

> No man can fully grasp how far and how fast we have come. But condense, if you will, the 50,000 years of man's recorded history into a time span of but a half-century. Stated in these terms, we know very little about the first 40 years, except that at the end of them advanced man had learned to use the skins of animals to cover himself. Then about 10 years ago, under this standard, man emerged from his caves to construct other kinds of shelter. Only 5 years ago, man learned to write and use a cart with wheels. Christianity began less than 2 years ago. The printing press came this year and then, less than 2 months ago, during this whole 50 year span of human history, the steam engine provided a new source of power. Last month electric lights and telephone and airplanes became available. Only last week did we develop penicillin and television and nuclear power. And now, if America's new spacecraft succeeds in reaching the stars, we will literally have reached the stars before midnight tonight. (Kennedy, 1962)

President Kennedy wondered at the breathtaking pace of it all.

If we extrapolate from the president's provocative scenario, we can infer that school reform had its genesis only a little more than two weeks ago and contemporary school design thinking and personalized instructional options are the work of this very hour. This whimsical timeline should cogently persuade us of the importance of assuring that school renewal is a work of the moment, a truly contemporary enterprise.

The need for change in our accustomed ways of schooling was evident to some educators as early as the last decades of the nineteenth century. We have been struggling with school renewal and restructuring for more than a century, yet we continue to conduct most schools today much as we did in that remote time. Today many still do not see the need for school change. They fail to see the benefit to society of schools that really meet the needs of *all* students. Indeed, most educators are not willing to assume the responsibilities that come with systemic school renewal, nor do they understand the *process* of change when renewal efforts are undertaken. Educators, parents, and policy makers are willing to talk about school reform, but do not want to act in ways that will prepare for its exigencies. We continue to be bogged down in a back-to-basics present that is really the distant past warmed over.

But make no mistake about our thinking on this important subject. The American public school system has been one of the world's spectacular success stories. The notion that every girl and boy, of whatever socioeconomic background, is entitled to equal educational opportunity is so startling that most of us who live in this society fail to appreciate its implications. Nowhere else in the world except for our neighbor and traditional partner, Canada, is there anything comparable to the American secondary system. And much of the rest of the world, seeing its validity and value, is following in our footsteps. In England, Germany, the Netherlands, Scandinavia, India, and Japan, attempts abound to imitate or duplicate the American model. That model is a deliberate attempt to educate the masses. At its best, it is an exemplar for the world. But it is not indestructible. It can and must continue to evolve to meet the needs of each succeeding generation. This kind of evolution cannot be accomplished by negativism or historicism, but by dedication, by commitment to the future, and by hard work.

Many attempts were made to change the direction of schooling during the twentieth century. House (1981), for example, describes three major perspectives on the school change process that are apparent in the research literature of the preceding 40 years:

- The Rational-Scientific or R & D Perspective that proposes to give educators valid information on improvements, which are subsequently implemented;
- The Political Perspective that mandates changes from the federal or state level or authorizes schools to make changes if certain conditions are met; and
- The Cultural Perspective, which maintains that improvements occur only with changes in values and expectations within schools or districts.

The R & D Perspective was dominant in the 1950s–1970s and proved to be naive. The Political Perspective was strong in the 1980s and resulted in a number of top-down initiatives that achieved very little. The Cultural Perspective flowing out of the school climate/culture movement and corporate sector impetus still influences contemporary efforts of school renewal (Keefe, Jenkins, & Hersey, 1992).

Sashkin and Egermeier (1991) argue that these trends have resulted in four broad strategies for changing schools, each with its own assumptions and action steps for change.

Strategy 1: Fix the parts by transferring innovations. Introduce specific new programs as the main thrust of school renewal. Offer start-up funding and technical assistance to help schools implement the innovations. This is the approach of the National Diffusion Network, which has piloted "exemplary programs" and supported efforts to implement them in schools. This approach borrows heavily from the "County Agent" model pioneered by the United States Department of Agriculture.

Strategy 2: Fix the people by training and developing professionals. This staff development strategy relies on in-service training to provide motivation, knowledge, and skills to administrators and teachers desirous of school change. The efforts of Madeline Hunter at the school level and the Holmes Group at the college level are well-known examples of this strategy.

Strategy 3: Fix the school by developing its capacities to solve problems. This is an organizational development (OD) approach in which a school is helped to become a better functioning organization. Schools collect data to identify problems and to evaluate whether solutions actually work. The intervention of outside experts is usually required for schools to rate their present levels of functioning. Substantial benefits can accrue, but the strategy can be costly and hence has not been widely implemented.

Strategy 4: Fix the system by comprehensive restructuring. This strategy proposes that schools adopt or adapt the best of innovative programs and staff development and organizational development strategies in a holistic approach that involves the individual school, the district, the community, and other pertinent agencies. It is a systemic approach that recognizes that the wider system can affect the change process within the local school. Comprehensive school renewal strategies like those of the Model Schools Project, the Learning Environments Consortium International, and the Coalition of Essential Schools reflect the wisdom of this strategy.

The process of school renewal has passed through several phases since the great period of school reform in the 1960s. The Model Schools Project (MSP, 1969–1974) was the culmination of much of the seminal thinking of that earlier era. "Staff Utilization Studies" sponsored by the National Association of Secondary School Principals (NASSP) in the 1950s led to the MSP, directed by J. Lloyd Trump, NASSP associate secretary for research and development, and partially funded by the Danforth Foundation. Thirty-six middle level and high schools participated in the NASSP Project with varying degrees of success. The Learning Environments Consortium International (LECI) was organized in 1974 as a limited follow-up to the MSP in the western regions of the United States and Canada. Learning Environments Consortium (LEC) is still functioning as the LEC Forum, a web-based organization of collaborating individuals dedicated to school design/ redesign and the personalization of instruction.

The climate for comprehensive school change altered in the 1970s with the competency-based movement, followed in turn by the Effective Schools movement and then by various back-to-basics initiatives. Theodore Sizer's Coalition of Essential Schools (CES) reinvigorated the push for comprehensive school renewal in the 1980s (through the present) by advancing a set of "essential principles" developed during a large-scale study of high schools. The Coalition has engaged some 1000 schools in comprehensive change, including those in the eight states of its Re:Learning initiative.

During this same period, the University of Wisconsin at Madison hosted two U.S. Department of Education research centers on the high school and school restructuring. The latter, the Center on Organization and Restructuring of Schools (CORS), collected and examined data from more than 1500 elementary, middle, and high schools throughout the United States and conducted field studies in 44 schools in 16 states. The Center's publications reported on what actually worked in school renewal and what types of human, social, and other resources were needed to support successful restructuring. The Center's proposal for success included emphasis on external support, school organizational capacity, what it called "authentic pedagogy," and the intellectual quality of student learning.

But even these kinds of comprehensive change efforts, no matter how sweeping, profound, or ideal, will remain barren unless they bring about changes in classroom routine in the ways that schools function and that students learn. If schooling is to expand its pedagogical horizons beyond the scope of the self-contained classroom, we must return to Plato's insight to employ the educational resources of the entire community. The school is the center of a wheel, a hub radiating out to all kinds of educational resources in the wider world. And we must learn once again from John Dewey to focus on the needs of individual students. This is a new and enhanced role for the school.

The process of school renewal has been going on for decades, with subsequent waves of reform and restructuring followed by equal or stronger movements of retrenchment. Much of the problem represented in this endless cycle can be explained by the woeful fact that the American public has never been willing to apply the canon of continual improvement to its schools. The problem is not that our schools have failed. Far from it. They still do well for the talented and the motivated. But they have become increasingly obsolete. The typical American public school curriculum and structure are more than 100 years old and are becoming more and more outdated. They were developed when the country primarily needed a blue-collar workforce and only a few students were expected to go to college. Some evolution has occurred and some significant, though piecemeal, changes have been made in this basic model of American schooling; but the core is relatively unchanged. Given these conditions, it is not difficult to understand why so many students today just coast through school. The majority simply want to pass through and avoid failing. Where grades and promotion to the next level are the prime goals not knowledge, skills, and understanding is it any wonder that so many students choose the path of least resistance?

Limited, small-scale change is much easier to plan and implement in schools, but the burden of more than nine decades of piecemeal efforts bears witness to the little success they engender. Unfortunately, even comprehensive change efforts have not had much long-term impact on what Tyack and Cuban (1995) call "the basic grammar of schooling." Perhaps the fault is in the imperfect institutionalization of these comprehensive initiatives, but more likely it lies with the expectations of a public that still expects schooling to look and feel like "what we went through," and the unwillingness of educators to exercise the leadership and exhibit the commitment needed for comprehensive change.

This book traces educational practice stemming from the NASSP Model Schools Project to the best in educational theory and practice today. Its bias lies with the comprehensive model of school change. Each chapter of the book focuses on a key concept of school renewal that was explicit or implicit in the MSP and describes what happened to it during the past 30 years. Did the concept survive as initially conceived, evolve into something meaningful for contemporary schools, or fail as so many other innovations have done? The chapter authors focus on the more substantial trends and the more comprehensive efforts of school renewal. The Model Schools Project set out deliberately to change "the basic grammar of schooling." This book attempts to determine whether and to what degree the project was successful.

CHAPTER 1

Comprehensive School Renewal: MSP, LEC, and CES

James W. Keefe

Home schooling and charter schooling are on the rise in the United States. A growing number of American parents—working to middle class, politically moderate, and unaffiliated with formal religious organizations—have taken over the education of their children because of frustration with conventional public schooling. These parents are not concerned only with public education's value orientation or the lack of a spiritual component, but with politically driven school boards, rigid district bureaucracies, curricula geared primarily to state testing, and class sizes that are still too large. They believe they can do better at home or in a local charter school that reflects their priorities. They want to provide their children with enriched environments, a wider range of experiences, and a more personal touch. Many, of course, are concerned about moral education, but an increasing number simply believe that typical public schools lack quality, safety, and personalization. The underlying message of the movement is clear: Public education is not meeting the needs of many students and families.

The challenge to mainstream public education from home schooling and charter schools is only a small dimension of a larger problem: How can all present-day schools provide an increasingly diverse student population with the knowledge and skills necessary to function in an increasingly global society? What kinds of school learning environments are best suited to the task? What forms of instruction are most likely to be successful in helping contemporary youth acquire problem-solving skills and sustain intrinsic motivation for learning? Can we continue to rely on the traditional classroom with its lockstep procedures, mind-numbing routines, and teacher domination? Very likely not! Can we, on the other hand, construct a highly personalized environment with sufficient structure and efficiency to shepherd thousands of youngsters from basic skills to higher order pursuits? Perhaps! English (1989), in writing about "A School for 2088," proposed a school environment in the form of an "educational colony." He conceived of this colony as a movie lot of learning experiences, with historical and linguistic immersion, curriculum as "scenario building" (replicas of various living environments of the past and present), and instruction through guiding and mentoring in a "fluid atmosphere" much like Epcot Center in Florida—all using technology available today. A challenging possibility!

We may not be quite ready yet for the school of 2088, but we can identify an intermediate stage of school renewal, beyond the traditional forms of most public schooling and the transitional approaches of "effective schooling" and individualized instruction. Are there truly interactive learning environments available out there that utilize the best of contemporary technology and pedagogy in an atmosphere of caring and support for individual learners? These environments would have to be flexible, but structured adequately to meet the needs of countless students. The organizational impact would have to be schoolwide—truly comprehensive in focus and scope.

Some schools have tried to develop comprehensive designs of their own, but more have looked to existing schoolwide reform programs for guidance. In 1991, former President George H. Bush challenged top American business leaders to back efforts to "break the mold" of a sluggish public school system with the energy of the private corporate sector. The New American Schools (NAS) program was established in that same year by the chief executives of America's most successful corporations. Under the direction of Xerox chairman emeritus, David Kearns, NAS was founded as a nonprofit organization with the mission to increase student achievement through comprehensive school improvement. NAS funded 11 "design teams" from among some 700 submitted proposals, including such distinguished programs as the Accelerated Schools Project and the ATLAS Communities (New American Schools Website, 2002). In 1998, the United States Congress voted $120 million to support comprehensive reform in Title I schools and $25 million for all public schools, with at least $50,000 going to individual selected schools. This Comprehensive School Reform Demonstration (CSRD) program required that schoolwide reform models promote high standards for all students, address all subject areas and grade levels, be research-based and -tested, share a common focus on goals, include professional development, align resources across grades and subject areas, and enable parent and community involvement (Education Commission of the States, 1998).

The potential for comprehensive school renewal is enormous if schools can overcome the initial hurdles of choosing and institutionalizing the best of contemporary school designs. Many are available. The so-called Obey-Porter list in the CSRD legislation cited 17 models that schools could adopt for funding. Some of the listed programs are still largely unproven, while others with proven success were omitted. The Obey-Porter list included such excellent programs as the K–8 Accelerated Schools Project (cited above), the Coalition of Essential Schools (K–12), and Paideia (K–12), but omitted such worthies as the Edison Schools (K–12), the Foxfire Fund (K–12), the Learning Environments Consortium International (K–12), and Montessori (preK–8) (see McChesney & Hertling, 2000, for these lists; descriptions of more reform models are available online at www.nwrel.org/scpd/natspec/catalog/index.html.) Similar exemplars are available in Canada, such as Michael Fullan's (1993) Learning Consortium for school-district "co-development" in Toronto and the Canadian Coalition for Self-Directed Learning Partnership of High Schools in Ontario, Alberta, and British Columbia.

Where can an interested school start the process of investigation and selection? In our alphabet-soup culture, no acronyms should be more meaningful to educators than MSP, LEC, and CES. These initials represent perhaps the most systematic and comprehensive examples of school renewal in the past three decades. The Model Schools Project (MSP, 1969–1974), sponsored by the National Association of Secondary School Principals, was the first comprehensive school reform venture of the second half of the twentieth century. Its follow-up in the western regions of the United States and Canada, the Learning Environments Consortium International, still functions today as a forum of educators dedicated to school redesign and the personalization of instruction in the United States and Canada. From the 1980s to the present, the CES engaged some

1000 American schools in attempts to redesign themselves in terms of its nine Common Principles, a set of broad, research-based criteria for school renewal. These three comprehensive school change initiatives have made a lasting impact on American and Canadian education. Let us see what the MSP, LEC, and CES can tell us about what is needed for the comprehensive renewal of schooling.

MODEL SCHOOLS PROJECT

Future historians of American education may well recognize J. Lloyd Trump, former associate secretary for research and development of the NASSP, as the pivotal school reform figure of the second half of the twentieth century (John Dewey is widely regarded as the pivotal figure of the first half). Trump headed the NASSP Commission on the Experimental Study of the Staff in the Secondary School in the 1950s. These so-called "Staff Utilization Studies" were the foundation of all of Trump's later work. During the 1960s and 1970s, Trump's contemporaries saw him as the leading authority on change in secondary education. His early work to redesign secondary schools became known as the "Trump Plan." Thousands of schools in the United States and Canada implemented the basic elements of the plan: team teaching, use of teacher assistants, large-group instruction, small-group instruction, independent study, flexible scheduling, and attention to student/teacher individual differences. During the late 1960s and early 1970s, Trump served as project director of the NASSP Model Schools Project, a national effort in some 36 American and Canadian schools to bring comprehensive, research-based change to middle-level and high school education.

For many decades, educators have relied heavily on large amounts of "prepackaging." Students were assumed to be ready for graded subject matter solely on the basis of age; blocks of information were assembled in textbooks geared to a nine-month school year; teachers were presumed to be universal experts in dealing with 25 to 40 students. Such assumptions ignored the fact that students learn at different rates and in unique ways; that learning should relate to the actual maturity and readiness of the learner and provide some personal satisfaction; and that teachers, like students, have special talents and weaknesses. A recognition of these realities led J. Lloyd Trump and his associate director of the Model Schools Project, William D. Georgiades of the University of Southern California, to postulate that truly significant change can take place in the school environment only when it occurs simultaneously in six broad areas: the role of the principal, teacher, student, curriculum, facilities, and evaluation. Trump and Georgiades proposed five basic principles for constructive change in secondary school operation:

- The school principal must devote a majority of his/her time to the improvement of instruction.
- The instructional staff must be reorganized using instructional aides to give teachers more freedom for instructional planning.
- Students need more time for independent study.
- The curriculum must offer continuous contact with essential materials in the basic areas of human knowledge.
- The "things of education"—buildings, equipment, supplies, and money—must be better utilized (Trump, 1969).

Teacher's Role

The role of the MSP teacher is central to an understanding of what the MSP considered meaningful for school reform. The Model describes the changing teacher role in these terms:

1. *Teacher-Advisor* (TA)—The MSP cast teachers in the role of advisor/counselor as well as subject matter facilitator. The teacher assumed responsibility for guiding 20 to 30 students in the formulation of their schedules, the organization of their independent study time (up to 20 hours per week), the assessment of their progress, and in assisting them with school adjustment problems. The TA role was the pivotal role for teachers in the project.
2. *Differentiated Staffing*—The MSP viewed teachers as functioning members of a team of professionals and paraprofessionals (aides) in which each member performed various tasks and assignments according to professional status and capabilities. Teachers were assisted by instructional, clerical, and general aides.
3. *Curriculum Design*—The MSP defined curriculum in terms of experiences and activities organized as basic, desirable, and enriching. The

basic program included experiences necessary for functional citizen-
ship. *Desirable* incorporated what was required for college preparation, vocational training, or personal interests. *Enriching* encom-
passed advanced work such as honors classes, advanced placement or
college courses, International Baccalaureate, etc.

4. *Learning Materials*—The school program was individualized in units
   and designed for continuous progress. Students worked through a series of learning guides that included varied resources such as books,
   media, models, teacher-prepared materials, and community and work
   experiences, as well as self-, pre-, and post-tests. Students completed
   learning sequences at their own pace, taking tests when they were
   ready to demonstrate mastery.
5. *Instructional Methods*—In the MSP, teachers planned large group
   presentations (LGP), motivational small group discussions (SGD),
   and independent study (IS) ("what students do when teachers stop
   talking"). The subject content was structured in continuous progress
   sequences of units or learning guides, with teachers providing diagnosis, prescription, instruction, and evaluation as appropriate.
6. *Student Grading*—The MSP asked schools and teachers to improve
   student evaluation by making less use of conventional alphanumeric
   grading and placing more emphasis on "what learners actually know
   and do." Progress reports rated students in terms of their own past
   achievement, their progress in the learning sequences, and their completion of special projects. (Trump, 1969, 1977)

The job of the teacher was greatly professionalized under this model.
Teachers served as teacher advisors for small groups of students during
their entire time at a school, prepared large group presentations and supervised small group discussions, and arranged their schedules to spe-
cialize in areas in which they had the most skill. Students, in turn, were
expected to take more responsibility for the success of their own education and generally to be more mature in their use of time, materials,
and equipment.

Impact of the MSP

Many schools embraced the ideas of the Trump Plan and the ensuing
MSP with few reservations, largely because of the cogency of its main
premise: Contemporary schools reflect a dated vision and organization

(that of the industrial revolution), and could and must change if they were to meet the needs of modern youth. Unfortunately, many schools did not sustain the vision. Success required commitment from the school board, superintendent, and community, strong principal leadership and change-agent skills, some seed money, and at least three to five years for implementation (and much longer for real institutionalization). Most schools lacked two or three of these institutional commitments and most principals were unable to provide the sustained leadership that was needed. In the long run, however, the major obstacles to the success of the MSP were a certain naiveté on the part of the project staff that one model of schooling was suitable for all schools, together with a concurrent back-to-basics backlash which simply overwhelmed any long-term influence the project might have had.

The MSP sponsored a considerable amount of formative evaluation but little summative evaluation. The project ultimately did not give the education community and the public the only kind of assurance that might have led to strong institutionalization of the concepts—compelling outcomes data. The desired goal of improving secondary education was clearly not achieved in the United States. In fact, the project had a much stronger impact on Canadian education. A number of the schools that still follow the original (or modified) model may be found in Canada.

The most important legacy of the MSP, however, was the educators it inspired who continued to develop its concepts and the subsequent reports and projects that it influenced. Many of the ideas in the Carnegie Foundation's *Turning Points* report (1989) and the NASSP/Carnegie *Breaking Ranks* report (1996) were contained or foreshadowed in the MSP. The LECI owes its origin directly to the MSP, and projects like IDEA Secondary and even the CES have their philosophical roots in the MSP. These connections are lost on many educators today who do not know the history of school reform. That unfortunate fact notwithstanding, the underlying concepts of the MSP continue to influence school renewal efforts well into the twenty-first century.

LEARNING ENVIRONMENTS CONSORTIUM INTERNATIONAL

The LECI is an independent, nonprofit organization pledged to assist interested schools in redesigning themselves and in developing personalized instructional programs. More than 25 years ago, at the conclusion of the MSP, representatives of five of the project's most successful schools (Chalmette, LA; Bakersfield, CA; Downey, CA; Everett, WA; and Calgary, Canada) met in Los Angeles with William Georgiades and Flavian Udinsky of the MSP staff to form a new organization. LECI was conceptualized in 1975 as a self-help consortium of *schools and districts*, initially in the western parts of the United States and Canada, dedicated to providing more responsive schooling for children and young people.

The consortium is committed to (a) a diagnostic-prescriptive paradigm of education, (b) a supervisory-management team approach to school administration with the principal serving as principal teacher and instructional leader, (c) a personalized strategy of instruction with teachers acting as learning facilitators and teacher advisers, and (d) systematic, performance-based evaluation of students, teachers, and program. LEC does not attempt to impose a rigid model on its participating organizations, because no one model of schooling is appropriate for all schools. Rather, it recommends altered administrative, teacher, and student roles and the personalization of instruction and assessment.

LEC worked directly with elementary and secondary school districts in the west for more than 20 years to design personalized schools. Then in 1996, LEC reconceptualized itself by broadening its original mission to embrace interested *individuals* with knowledge and experience in the research and practice of school renewal. The LEC Forum operates on a pro-bono basis within the structure of LECI, with members contributing ideas and time toward its defined goals. The Forum agenda focuses on information dissemination through publications and workshops, with some direct assistance to interested schools.

Administrative Role

Enhanced building-level leadership is a sine qua non in LEC schools. Drawing on its MSP origins, LEC sees the principal as the pivotal figure in school change and contends that if instruction is to improve, principals must work directly with teachers toward that goal. The instructional program, rather than management of the organization and its buildings, is the principal's primary responsibility. The principal's role in LEC schools is one of "teacher of teachers." The principal in turn is closely connected to teachers through the supervisory-management team (SMT) that serves as the linchpin for school and staff communication. The SMT is composed of administrator, teacher, and sometimes student representatives who meet regularly with the principal, and it acts as the school leadership unit. The role of the principalship is greatly enlarged through this SMT collaboration.

Personalized Education

The need to personalize education for all learners remains a significant challenge to contemporary educators. Personalized education begins with the learner and builds the learning environment on learner needs and interests. The instructional design recommended by the LEC is the DPIE Model: diagnosis, prescription, implementation, and evaluation. The Consortium advocates this model because research and practice support its positive correlation with student achievement. The personalized education model (see Figure 1.1) was formulated, initially in the 1970s, specifically for LECI (Keefe, 1989; Keefe & Jenkins, 2000).

LEC schools have applied the personalized education model in various ways, from a complete continuous progress curriculum to school-within-school applications, to learning team, contract learning, and project approaches. Personalization focuses on the learner. It is "an attempt to achieve a balance between the characteristics of the learner and the learning environment" (Carroll, 1975). It is a

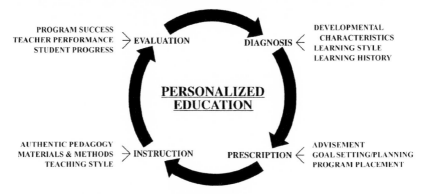

Figure 1.1. *Model of Personalized Education*

process of adaptation. Program offerings are personalized to meet learner needs. A key element is the interaction between teacher and student.

The LEC personalized approach to instruction is characterized by:

1. A *dual teacher role* of coach and adviser.
2. The *diagnosis* of relevant student learning characteristics, including developmental level, cognitive/learning style, and prior knowledge/ skills (learning history).
3. A *culture of collegiality* in the school, characterized by a constructivist environment and collaborative learning arrangements.
4. An *interactive learning environment*, characterized by small school or small group size, thoughtful conversation, active learning activities, and authentic student achievement.
5. *Flexible scheduling and pacing*, but with adequate structure.
6. *Authentic assessment* (Keefe & Jenkins, 2000).

SCHOOL DESIGN/REDESIGN

The LECI is especially distinguished by its commitment to the process of total school design/redesign. Contemporary schools for the most part have just evolved from earlier forms of schooling, with little thought given to the validity or relevance of the organizational structures and programs. LECI believes that schools interested in systematic improvement must first become learning organizations and develop their own "School Design Statements," with carefully *written specifications* for the design components. School design applies systems thinking to the process of school renewal.

The LEC School Design Statement consists of:

A. Three Basic Components
   1. Mission and Vision Statements
   2. Culture and Climate Statements
   3. Student Goals and Outcomes
B. Eight Systemic Components
   1. Curriculum and Instructional Program
   2. Instructional Techniques

3. School Structure and Organization
4. School Leadership, Management, and Budgeting
5. School Staffing and Staff Development
6. Communication and Political Structures
7. School Resources, Physical Plant, and Equipment
8. Evaluation Plan
C. Specifications for Each Component

LEC advocates a School Improvement Process developed by Keefe and Howard (1997) for the NASSP. The process involves the formation of a School Management/Design Team (SM/DT) that conducts awareness, commitment, and development activities and works with the staff to create a school learning organization. The SM/DT initiates the planning process by collecting and analyzing school data and undertaking a literature search to determine the direction and scope of the school design/redesign. The team then guides the school staff in developing the basic and systemic components of the School Design Statement and writing specifications for each of its components. The final phases of the design involve preparing an action plan with task force formation, priority-setting steps for each component of the design, and evaluation and reporting processes. The design/redesign process typically takes three to five years depending on the readiness of the school and community and the available resources. The value of such a statement is incontestable; it constitutes a blueprint for all to see of the future parameters of the school.

COALITION OF ESSENTIAL SCHOOLS

Many policy makers and members of the public were concerned with the direction of public education in the 1970s. Many believed that the wave of educational innovations of the late 1950s and the 1960s might be to blame for what were perceived as reduced academic standards and school discipline, falling SAT scores and reading levels, and a general absence in the student and adult population of the minimal skills needed to cope in modern society. A "back to basics" backlash began to develop steam, with emphasis on the three "Rs" and such parallel movements as

Competency-Based Education (CBE), Management by Objectives (MBO), and corporate-based school performance contracting.

But comprehensive school reform did not entirely languish during this period. From 1966–1971, the Institute for Development of Educational Activities (IDEA) sponsored a network of 18 schools in Southern California called the League of Cooperating Schools under the leadership of educational pioneer John Goodlad (1975). The League provided a clearinghouse of innovative ideas and practices for its members—a meeting place for discussion and problem solving. In the same time period, IDEA backed the development of Individually Guided Education (IGE) through the work of the Wisconsin Research and Development Center, later the Wisconsin Center for Education Research (WCER). The IGE program was IDEA's change program for schools, "not a curriculum, [but] a system for organizing and delivering educational experience" (IDEA Website, 2002). IGE advocated a diagnostic-prescriptive approach to learning and instruction with teachers as advisors and facilitators and the entire school community involved as supportive participants—all basic Model Schools Project concepts.

The benefits of contemporary over traditional approaches to education were confirmed by many studies published from the 1960s through the mid-1980s. Kohn (1999) points out that

> a review of some 57 studies of "activity-based" and "process-oriented" elementary school science programs (in which no textbooks were used, by the way) found that students emerged as much better thinkers than their counterparts in traditional classrooms—and they didn't sacrifice any learning of basic content. The benefit of the nontraditional instruction in these studies was especially significant for disadvantaged students.

Regrettably, high school studies emphasizing meaning and understanding were scarce in this period because so few high school classes then were truly student-centered. But the WCER and its CORS changed all that in the 1980s and 1990s by conceptualizing and studying the notions of student engagement and "authentic learning" and developing evidence from middle and high school as well as elementary levels of schooling.

The CORS studies of school restructuring from 1990–1995 focused on student learning—to discover how the various tools of restructuring could improve learning for all students. The Center found no panacea, but noted that school restructuring "advanced student learning when it concentrated on the intellectual quality of student work, when it built school wide organizational capacity to deliver authentic pedagogy, and when it received support from the external environment that was consistent with these challenges" (Newmann & Wehlage, 1995). CORS scholars argued that pedagogy is authentic when it is based on the type of mastery demonstrated by successful adults in all walks of life. In the real world, *people actually do things*; they solve problems, create knowledge or products, and resolve controversies. Authentic assessment, in turn, uses real performance or products to establish mastery, not just grades or some other measure to indicate rank or completion of a learning segment (Keefe & Jenkins, 2000).

The research of the CORS added weight to the efforts of the CES. The coalition was founded in 1984 at Brown University by the eminent educator Theodore R. Sizer, following a large-scale research project, A Study of High Schools, and a series of books discussing the results. In 1979, Sizer, former dean of the Harvard Graduate School of Education and former headmaster of Phillips Academy-Andover, wanted to better understand American secondary education. Sizer summarized his study in the first of three books about the project, *Horace's Compromise: The Dilemma of the American High School* (1984) and later published *Horace's School* (1992) and *Horace's Hope* (1996) to further describe what works and what doesn't work in the process of change at the local high school level. The coalition is a

national network of schools, regional centers, and a national office, working to create schools where intellectual excitement animates every child's face, where teachers work together to get better at their craft, and where all children flourish, regardless of their gender, race, or class. (CES National Website, 2002a)

The Coalition network in 2002 consisted of about 800 schools and 18 regional centers that provided information and coaching services to schools. Schools can be certified to receive Comprehensive School

Reform Demonstration funds if they are affiliated with a CES regional center.

Like LECI and the CSRD, the Coalition rejects the notion of a "one size fits all" model for all schools. It supports the concept of *shared ideas* that good schools have in common about learning and schooling. Sizer summarized his views of these shared ideas as a set of common principles—beliefs about the purpose and practice of schooling. In slightly abbreviated form, the principles for elementary and secondary schools are as follows:

1. The school should focus on helping young people learn to use their minds well. Schools should not be "comprehensive" if such a claim is made at the expense of the school's central intellectual purpose.
2. The school's goals should be simple: that each student masters a limited number of essential skills and areas of knowledge. . . . The aphorism "less is more" should dominate: Curricular decisions should be guided by the aim of thorough student mastery and achievement rather than by an effort to merely cover content.
3. The school's goals should apply to all students, while the means to these goals will vary as those students themselves vary. School practice should be tailor-made to meet the needs of every group or class of students.
4. Teaching and learning should be personalized to the maximum feasible extent. Efforts should be directed toward a goal that no teacher have direct responsibility for more than 80 students in the high school and no more than 20 in the elementary school. To capitalize on this personalization, decisions about the details of the course of study, the use of students' and teachers' time, and the choice of teaching materials and specific pedagogies must be unreservedly placed in the hands of the principal and staff.
5. The governing practical metaphor of the school should be student-as-worker, rather than the more familiar metaphor of teacher-as-deliverer-of-instructional-services. Accordingly, a prominent pedagogy will be coaching, to provoke students to learn how to learn and thus to teach themselves.
6. Teaching and learning should be documented and assessed with tools based on student performance of real tasks. . . . Multiple forms of evidence, ranging from ongoing observation of the learner to completion of specific projects, should be used. . . . The diploma

should be awarded upon a successful demonstration of mastery for graduation—an "Exhibition." . . . The school's program proceeds with no strict age grading and with no system of "credits earned" by "time spent" in class.

7. The tone of the school should explicitly and self-consciously stress values of unanimous expectation, of trust . . . and of decency. . . . Incentives appropriate to the school's particular students and teachers should be emphasized. Parents should be key collaborators and vital members of the school community.

8. The principal and teachers should perceive themselves as generalists first (teachers and scholars in general education) and specialists second (experts in but one particular discipline). Staff should expect multiple obligations (teacher-counselor-manager) and a sense of commitment to the whole school.

9. Ultimate administrative and budget targets should include . . . substantial time for collective planning by teachers, competitive salaries for staff, and ultimate per pupil cost not to exceed that at traditional schools by more than 10 percent. To accomplish this, administrative plans may have to show the phased reduction or elimination of some services.

10. The school should demonstrate non-discriminatory and inclusive policies, practices, and pedagogies. It should model democratic practices that involve all who are directly affected by the school. The school should honor diversity and build on the strength of its communities, deliberately and explicitly challenging all forms of inequality. (CES National Website, 2002b)

The "essential" in the CES title means that coalition schools "focus on a few of the most essential things and meet them head on, instead of trying to do and be everything" (Dykema, 2002). The Coalition calls for the development of small schools and classrooms, democratic and equitable school policies, personalized instruction to meet individual student needs, assessments requiring performance of authentic tasks, and close partnerships with parents and community. The common principles are a guide for local schools "in setting priorities and designing practice, as each school develops its own programs, suited to its particular students, faculty, and community" (CES National Website, 2002a).

Many CES schools also utilize the standards and practices of "authentic pedagogy" derived from the University of Wisconsin's CORS research. Authentic instruction and assessment move CES schools to focus on depth of knowledge and "thoughtfulness" rather than broad coverage of content, on cultivating the roles of "student as worker" and "teacher as coach," and on establishing a personalized learning environment based on strong working relationships between students and teachers.

> The task of the Essential School is to adapt—to personalize—its program so that each student, or small group of students, can "elect" the means to that essential end, however discouraging that goal may appear at first. . . . Schools must be personalized to the maximum feasible extent (Sizer, 1984).

Again like LECI, the Coalition urges "school design," not just the physical design and use of the building but a series of decisions about school organizational and instructional capacity—staffing, course offerings, time management, instructional strategies, community involvement, and so forth. Simon (1999) asserts that

> there is no single blueprint for the design of a great school, because great schools respond to the particular contexts and needs of their communities. The research and experience of the Coalition demonstrates, however, that there are four elements that all excellent schools share and that are essential for making significant, lasting improvements in student achievement and in creating a nurturing school culture. The four elements are as follows:

> 1. Course and curriculum must be designed so that all students are required to do serious intellectual work.
> 2. Students must be known well. The student to teacher ratio must not exceed 80:1 in secondary schools or 20:1 in elementary schools, and teachers and students must spend extended time together during the day and over the weeks and years.
> 3. Teachers must have substantial authority over their work, must have time to collaborate, and must have shared groups of students for whom they take responsibility.
> 4. Family and community involvement must be expected and cultivated.

Theodore Sizer and his wife, Nancy, one year into retirement, served as co-principals of a CES charter school in central Massachusetts, Parker Central School, which they helped to found. The school draws students from 55 Massachusetts cities and towns and is a delightful example of what an essential school can be. The school is organized into three divisions (7–8, 9–10, 11–12) and the program integrates the school disciplines under three academic domains: the arts and humanities (including Spanish language); mathematics, science, and technology; and health and adventure. The coursework each year centers on an "essential question," such as "What is change?" or "What is balance?" Teachers address the question at all levels of the school and generate sub-questions that concern content knowledge and skills. The result is an inquiry-based process that emphasizes thoughtful conversation and problem solving. Standards exist for each content area in each division. Students advance through the divisions by completing "Gateway Portfolios" and graduate by creating a "Capstone Senior Project" with a public presentation or exhibition of their knowledge and skills. Parker Central School neither assigns traditional grades nor ranks its students. Teachers assess student work in narrative reports keyed to the division standards (Keefe & Jenkins, 2000).

The Coalition takes both intellectual challenge and personalization very seriously. CES schools employ strategies originally developed in the progressive education era of the 1920s and 1930s as well as some of the best ideas of the 1960s and 1970s. The CES newsletter *Horace* cites Coalition schools using such vintage reform tactics as thematic (unit) workshops, as well as block-of-time-scheduling, teacher teaming, school-within-school organization, and cross-age grouping of students, in addition to contemporary strategies like authentic pedagogy. The Coalition has incorporated much of what has gone before, framed these ideas within its common-sense and concise philosophical principles, and amplified them with innovative contemporary strategies.

RETROSPECTIVE

This first chapter attempts to establish a broad outline of educational trends set in motion by the NASSP MSP almost 35 years ago and continued through many initiatives to the present. We cite two comprehensive projects of the past three decades in some detail: the LECI and the CES. To what extent have the MSP initiatives endured? This question will be answered in more detail in subsequent chapters. Here we simply establish the MSP benchmark concepts and some of the major trends advanced by LEC and CES.

The Model Schools Project proposed several key innovations:

- *Main Concept*: Total commitment to total change will produce better teaching and learning.
- *Curriculum Content*: Differentiated according to (a) basic (essential) for all students to know in all subject areas, (b) desirable (elective), and (c) enriching (career-oriented). Curriculum must offer "continuous contact" with essential materials in all the basic areas.
- *Instructional Methods*: Large group presentation, small group discussion, independent study, and continuous progress arrangements in a non-graded, non-time-sequenced scheduling process.
- *Locus of Teaching and Learning*: Study and work centers in the school, suitable arrangements in the community, and home study when appropriate.
- *Evaluation of Student Progress*: Periodic reports to parents on student progress in completing required learning sequences, on test scores both standardized and local, and on what each student achieves beyond the required sequences, whether academic or co-curricular.
- *Evaluation of the Total School Program*: Changes in pupil roles and behaviors, in teaching and supervisory roles, in parent and community perceptions of the school, and in the utilization of school, community, and home resources.
- *Differentiated Instructional Staff*: Teachers released from many clerical and general supervisory duties; instructional, clerical, and general assistants provided, up to 35 hours per week based on student-teacher ratios for the entire school.
- *Differentiated Counseling Staff*: Teacher advisors to monitor the schedules, progress, and *educational* problems of about 30 students; professional counselors to help students with *personal*

problems and work with about 15 teacher advisors and their advisees; special consultants brought in as needed.

- *Differentiated Supervisory/Management Staff*: Principal to spend three-fourths of his/her time on instructional improvement; an assistant principal for instruction for each 1000 students; others such as the Building Administrator, External Relations Director, Personnel Administrator, and Activities Director to oversee the other supervisory/management functions of the school.
- *Time management*: Continuous progress scheduling in the hands of teacher advisors; teacher schedules arranged jointly by teachers, department chairs, and the principal.
- *Numbers*: Large groups of 40 to 100 in each subject for about 30 minutes each week; small groups of 15 to 20 soon after LGPs for about 30 minutes of reaction discussion; other numbers for independent study, tutorial, and seminars vary with purpose and location.
- *Spaces*: Size, type, and locale to vary with purpose.
- *Money*: Financial input analyzed in terms of product-output; better accountability by producing better outcomes from present expenditures.
- *Other Options*: Procedures not just routine, but defensible alternatives of all kinds permitted—in learning strategies, types of study and work centers, their locations, progress reporting arrangements, scheduling and graduation options, etc. (NASSP, 1969).

The LECI as the direct but unofficial successor of the MSP has retained many of its key concepts to this day. LEC supports the main MSP concept of total school design/redesign, as well as the concepts of essential learning, multiple methodologies and locales for learning, more effective forms of student assessment and progress reporting, total school evaluation, a dual teacher role of coach and adviser, a differentiated supervisory-management team with the principal as instructional leader, and the better use of "the things of education." Specifics—such as the three MSP levels of curriculum differentiation, continuous contact with all the basic areas of curriculum, time-based allocation of large group, small group, and independent study strategies, continuous progress scheduling, and the systematic use of instructional assistants—have been abandoned or vary widely in LEC schools.

The CES also owes much to the MSP. The Coalition is strongly committed to the MSP concept of comprehensive school design/redesign and to the primacy of essential learning's broad coverage of content. It supports more effective forms of student assessment, progress reporting and total school evaluation, a dual teacher role of coach and adviser, and the more productive use of the "things of education." It does not employ the MSP's approaches to curriculum content and continuous contact with all basic areas, the specific mix of LGP/SGD/IS instructional methods, continuous progress scheduling, or differentiated staff and administration.

Precisely and to what degree LEC, CES, and other contemporary initiatives have retained the original MSP concepts or have fashioned a new and authentic rationale is the subject matter of the remaining chapters of this book.

CHAPTER 2

Role of the Principal and Supervisory-Management Team

Ronald G. Joekel

The role of the school principal or head teacher was one of the first positions that appeared in the realm of administration in schools. The position emerged as schools became large enough to warrant more than one teacher and governing bodies began to appoint a "head teacher" (Brubacher, 1947). Prior to the appointment of "head teachers" or "principal teachers," many one-room schools existed where the teacher was responsible for everything. With the growth of urban centers, schools not only increased in size but also in complexity to the point where governing boards felt the need to have someone in charge.

From this humble beginning, the role of the school principal has evolved and the success of a school is tied to the leadership of the principal and the competency and collaboration of the administrative team and faculty. The results of research support the conclusion that strong leadership by the school principal is essential for achieving educational excellence. Comparative research of effective and less effective inner-city schools, for example, has highlighted strong leadership of the principal as a vital characteristic of schools of quality (Edmonds, 1979).

MODEL SCHOOLS PROJECT

The role of the principal has changed profoundly over the years. Early responsibilities involved discipline and keeping records as well as a full-time teaching load. As student populations increased and schools grew, the principal taught fewer classes and assumed more management duties. As schools became more complex, the addition of assistant principals followed. The NASSP under the leadership of J. Lloyd Trump identified the complex role of the principal as becoming bogged down in "administravia." In a film produced by Trump in 1966 to mark the 50th anniversary of the NASSP, a typical day in the life of a principal was portrayed. It showed the principal greeting teachers and students, checking all kinds of building situations, and handling one crisis after another throughout the day. At the end of the day, the film showed the principal picking up some paper off the floor and turning out the lights after the PTA meeting. The question was posed: "Everything that he did had to be done, but did it have to be done by him?" (Trump, 1977). Trump recommended the supervisory-management team concept be implemented to provide more time for the principal to be the instructional leader.

THE SUPERVISORY-MANAGEMENT TEAM

The MSP proposed a team approach for secondary schools to meet the challenges of the 1970s. The following supervisory-management positions and a brief description were developed by the MSP (Trump, 1977).

School Principal: The principal is the head of the team and needs to spend about quarter of the time supervising, coordinating, and working closely with other members. The principal is liaison to the superintendent and the central office supervisors. He also coordinates relationships with external groups. The majority of the principal's time is spent directly on the improvement of instruction with department heads and teachers.

Assistant Principal: This person may be full-time or part-time based upon the size of the school. However, the assistant principal should be working collaboratively with the principal on instructional improvement.

Building Administrator: Supervision of the general office, the cafeteria, physical facilities, and transportation systems are the main responsibilities of this person.

External Relations Director: Among the duties of this person are translating the school's financial needs into written proposals to the central office, all levels of governmental agencies, foundations, and other appropriate groups. This person also has responsibility for the school's public relations program.

Personnel Administrator: This team member supervises attendance, discipline, and guidance. Responsibilities include working with teachers, students, parents, and other persons having problems or concerns with school youth. This person is also the liaison with other community youth-serving agencies.

Activities Director: Responsibilities include the development and supervision of student and faculty activities, including the supervision of athletic and non-athletic programs and social events. Scheduling school facilities both within the school and to external groups fall into this person's responsibility.

Department Chairpersons: These persons have major responsibility for curriculum development and implementation in their area of academic specialization. Typically there are eight curriculum areas but depending upon the school philosophy they may be combined in some cases, especially in smaller schools.

Regardless of the size of the school, the principal must assess the tasks to be done and develop a collaborative group to do them. Principals have the responsibility to know and plan the directions of the program. In the MSP many of the principal's efforts were directed through the Supervisory Management Team members, who were to meet regularly to assess needs, develop programs, and evaluate results. Georgiades (1991) portrayed the SMT as a differentiated staffing approach that acknowledged the importance of school management, but also recognized that the principal cannot do it alone. The SMT directed school personnel in conducting local studies that provided quality information about the home, the community, and the school. The major focus of these studies was to be on people and their aspirations and concerns. Of course the composition of the team varied with the size of the school and the variety of school programs.

Ideas growing out of these studies were shared with others and illustrations of already successful strategies and ideas were used as a motivational means for participants. The SMT led discussion groups to bring about plans for implementation and evaluation.

The SMT facilitated the group process with interested teachers, students, and community persons, opening the door for new ideas and strategies. The SMT operated in a manner to keep key people informed, and it made certain that everyone knew what was going on.

The SMT helped to create a school and community environment that gave new ideas and programs a chance to be successful. When programs were underway, the SMT visited the places where teaching and learning took place, especially where help was needed. Innovative teachers and students were encouraged, and they met frequently to discuss what they were doing and how it was working. Differentiated staff arrangements made time available for these meetings. The SMT met regularly with teachers and students, redefining goals and helping participants collect authentic data that measured the results accurately (Trump, 1977). It is interesting that the term "authentic assessment" was used by Trump in the MSP in the 1960s, long before the term became a buzzword in educational circles in the 1990s (when standards and assessment took over the conversation). Ironically, the "No Child Left Behind" legislation of the Bush administration in 2002 focused heavily on "assessment" and "standards," which were key concepts of the MSP.

A number of events have transpired since the MSP of 1969 that have modified the concept of the SMT. Growing out of research on organizational development have been such concepts as site-based management, shared decision making, empowerment, graded/non-graded organization, school-within-a school, and learning communities. With each new concept there has been an accompanying definition of administrative roles. Of the seven positions developed in the MSP SMT, four have remained fairly constant over time. They are the School Principal, Assistant Principal, Activities Director, and Department Chairpersons. The duties of the three other positions have been subsumed under a variety of different arrangements including adding additional assistant principals in larger schools with specific duties, the development of a Director of Guidance and Counseling position, and the use of Deans-Coordinators-Supervisors-Directors with specific assigned duties. Probably the most significant event that has transpired since the MSP is a paradigm shift from the concept of an SMT to the School Leadership Team (SLT).

ROLE OF THE PRINCIPAL

Research on management, leadership, and the role and duties of the school principal have led to the SLT model with emphasis on the Principal and Assistant Principal positions at the building level. There have been a number of studies on the principal and many have focused on the daily life of the "typical" principal (Wolcott, 1973), the position as a key ingredient in effective schools (Lipham, 1981), and how individuals might be more adequately prepared to step into that role (Gresso, 1986; Murphy, 1992).

The age-old question "Is a school principal a manager or a leader?" was best answered by Bennis (1989), when he said:

> The manager administers; the leader innovates. The manager has a short-range view; the leader has a long-range perspective. The manager asks how and when; the leader asks what and why. The manager accepts the status quo; the leader challenges it. The manager does things right; the leader does the right thing.

Arygris (1982) suggests that the job of manager is to keep things moving correctly according to the norms that have already been set. Management works from a perspective of "problem solving" with scant attention given to raising questions about the appropriateness of established norms. Ubben, Hughes, and Norris (2001) believe that the notion of leadership is much different. They contend that leaders build on the status quo but go well beyond it. A leader continually reexamines the norm to determine if what the organization is doing is what it should be doing. Foster (1984) stated, "Leaders always have one face turned toward change." Leaders go beyond problem solving to engage in problem finding. Principals not only manage, they also lead with a leadership perspective.

Beck and Murphy (1993), in studying the literature on the role of the principal over the past 70 years, used metaphors to describe how the role of the building level administrator has changed:

1. The 1920s and the 1930s
   - *The principal as spiritual leader.* The work of the principal was linked with absolute, spiritual truths and values.
   - *The principal as scientific manager.* The principalship is energized by a zeal for education and guided by the principles of scientific management.

- *The principal as social leader.* The principal is expected to be a social leader in the community.
- *The principal as dignified leader.* In all cases, principals act with dignity and importance.

2. The 1940s
   - *The principal as the leader on the home front.* During World War II, the principal is the school's leader at home.
   - *The principal as democratic leader.* The principal is expected to demonstrate democratic leadership.
   - *The principal as curriculum leader, group coordinator, and supervisor.* The principal is directly involved with the school's instructional program.
   - *The principal as public relations representative.* The principal communicates practices and priorities of the school to the community.

3. The 1950s
   - *The principal as administrator.* The principal is seen as a person who can bring together the worlds of effective teaching and management.
   - *The principal as defender of educational practice.* The principal defends the work of educators by offering empirical evidence of effective performance.
   - *The principal as efficient manager of time.* The principal is involved with prioritizing organizational tasks so that everything desired can be accomplished.
   - *The principal as overseer of minute details.* The principal gets involved with all matters related to school operation, whether large or small.

4. The 1960s
   - *The principal as bureaucrat.* The principal is a member of a well-developed educational bureaucracy, with clearly defined bases of power and responsibility.
   - *The principal as protector of bureaucracy.* The principal guards the distribution of power within the hierarchy and handles those who challenge the system.
   - *The principal as user of scientific strategies.* The principal uses empirical data in planning and measuring the work of the school and teachers.
   - *The principal as accountable leader.* The principal is held accountable for measurable outcomes in the school.

- *The principal as inhabitant of a role in conflict.* The principal lives in a state of confusion over what his or her role is to be in reality.
5. The 1970s
   - *The principal as community leader.* The principal is expected to lead students, teachers, and the larger community as well.
   - *The principal as the imparter of meaning.* The principal is supposed to impart meaning to educational efforts.
   - *The principal as juggler of multiple roles.* The principal is expected to juggle a number of roles that often require competing skills.
   - *The principal as facilitator of positive relationships.* The principal is expected to relate well to persons and to facilitate positive interactions between students and teachers.
6. The 1980s
   - *The principal as problem solver and resource provider.* The principal solves problems and provides resources to facilitate the teaching and learning process.
   - *The principal as instructional leader.* The principal is expected to guide teachers and students toward productive learning experiences.
   - *The principal as visionary.* The principal is expected to develop and communicate a picture of the ideal school.
   - *The principal as change agent.* The principal is expected to facilitate needed changes in educational operations to ensure school effectiveness.
7. The 1990s
   - *The principal as leader.* The principal is to lead the transition from a bureaucratic model of schooling to a postindustrial model.
   - *The principal as servant.* The principal provides direction for change while not offending the integrity of the hierarchical structure of school systems.
   - *The principal as organizational architect.* The principal must find ways for schools to exist productively within their natural environments.
   - *The principal as educator.* The principal returns to an earlier image as the primary teacher in the schools.
   - *The principal as moral agent.* The principal serves as values analyst and witness to lead the ethical formation of the school community.
   - *The principal as person in the community.* The principal leads the school as part of a caring and integrated community.

As we enter the 2000s, we are starting to see a drifting away from an emphasis on principals serving as teachers and more emphasis on the role of principals in reacting to the standards movement and accountability concerns. The greatest incursion of the federal government into public education, highlighted by the "No Child Left Behind Act" of 2002, is redefining the role of principals: More attention is focused on aligning curriculum to state standards and on developing and implementing assessment measures to demonstrate competence of students in meeting those standards.

RESEARCH FINDINGS ON THE EFFECTIVENESS OF THE PRINCIPAL

For many years the prevailing view of the principalship centered around principals' preparation for managerial tasks or on the development of conceptual skills borrowed from the social sciences. John Daresh (2002) described these two views as follows: One perspective emphasized the business of keeping an organization headed in the right direction by making certain that operational details were addressed, while the other perspective emphasized that a principal needed to be able to appreciate the way things work in an organization so that it might be possible to intervene when necessary. The books *Administrative Theory in Education*, edited by Andrew Halpin (1958), and *Educational Administration as a Social Process*, by Jacob Getzels, James Lipham, and Ronald Campbell (1968), have served for many years as influential and visible statements of the belief that the world of administration is not simply about "doing things" but, more important, about being able to "understand and explain" things that happen in the daily lives of schools.

There is a plethora of research on principal effectiveness. For many years it has been proposed that "as the principal goes so goes the school," and numerous research studies substantiate this statement. Sweeny (1982) summarized research studies concerning the school principal and concluded that there are certain leadership behaviors and specific activities that seem to make a difference. He found that effective principals made student achievement their top priority. He further found that some of the specific activities of successful principals include scheduling faculty meetings to discuss student achievement, reducing classroom interruptions, using student assemblies and exhibits to reward student achievement, sharing information about academic achievement with students, faculty, and citizens, and highlighting the significance of achievement to students.

Reilly (1984) reported that effective principals focused on student achievement and that they had high expectations of faculty and students while providing strong leadership in developing instructional goals and means for evaluating outcomes.

Andrews and Soder (1987) conducted research focusing on how the presence of strong leadership impacted the performance of students. Using teachers in the Seattle, Washington, school district as subjects, Andrews and Soder administered a questionnaire looking at interactions that occur between principals and teachers. The questionnaire measured these interactions in four areas: (a) the principal as resource provider, (b) the principal as instructional resource, (c) the principal as communicator, and (d) the principal as visible presence. Their findings showed that the normal equivalent-gain scores of students in schools led by strong instructional leaders (as perceived by the teachers) were significantly greater in both total reading and total mathematics than those of students in schools rated as having average or weak leaders (as perceived by the teachers).

Hallinger and Heck (1996), synthesizing 15 years of research on how principals impact their schools, reported that principals exercise a measurable, though indirect, effect on school effectiveness and student achievement.

Educational Research Service (2000), in a report prepared for the National Association of Elementary School Principals and the NASSP, concluded that the impact of principal leadership on student achievement is a compelling one: If you want to have an effective school characterized by teachers and students who are dedicated to learning, become a strong instructional leader.

Leithwood and Montgomery (1982) reported that effective principals saw themselves as instructional leaders providing the best possible programs for students. Most of the research findings in the literature strongly imply that the principal is the important person in providing leadership for improved instruction and better curricula (Kimbrough & Burkett, 1990).

PRINCIPAL TASKS AND SKILLS

There has been about as much written concerning the tasks carried out by principals and the skills needed as there has been on research studies describing the work of the principal. Hughes and Ubben (1984) identified five areas in which the principal must function effectively: (a) school-community relations, (b) staff personnel development, (c) pupil personnel development, (d) educational program development, and (e) business and building management. The NASSP Assessment Center project, directed by Paul Hersey, identified essential abilities needed by school principals to deal with the myriad of responsibilities they face (Hersey, n.d.). Among these essential abilities are problem analysis, judgment, organizational ability, decisiveness, leadership, sensitivity, range of interests, personal motivation, stress tolerance, educational values, oral communication, and written communication.

A series of new efforts to look at the school principal began in the 1980s, with the U.S. Department of Education program for improvement of preparation programs for school administrators (mostly principals) called Leadership in Educational Administration Development (LEAD). Eight leadership skills were identified for the project: (a) creating and enhancing a schoolwide environment that promotes learning and student achievement; (b) evaluating the school curriculum in order to assess and improve its effectiveness in meeting academic and other goals; (c) analyzing, evaluating, and improving instruction and teacher performance; (d) appraising and assessing student performance and other indicators of overall school performance; (e) understanding and applying the findings of research to school leadership and improvement; (f) organizing and managing school resources; (g) ensuring student discipline and a climate of order; and (h) developing human relations skills.

The Danforth Program for the Preparation of School Principals developed from a position paper in 1987 that had a major impact on the preparation of school principals. The program developed a partnership between university professors and public school administrators, with emphasis on experiential learning situations such as simulated activities and self-study activities. The focus on experiential learning was designed to allow candidates to demonstrate competencies in schools and communities beyond those commonly expressed in schools at the time, according to the Danforth Foundation.

The NASSP and the National Association of Elementary Schools appointed a national commission to study the preparation and certification of school principals, reflecting not only the theory-based constructs of preparation but also the real world of practitioners. The result was the publication of *The Principals for Our Changing Schools: Preparation and Certification* (National Commission for the Principalship, 1990). Twenty-one domains were identified by the commission as being essential areas of knowledge and skills of school principals.

In 1993, the National Policy Board for Educational Administration came forth with the book *Principals for Our Changing Schools: Knowledge and Skill Base,* which built upon the 21 domains identified by the joint commission. McCall (1994) professed that until 1993, no one had really done the basic research to answer the question of, "What essential knowledge and skills do school principals need to function effectively?" In the preface to McCall's book, editor Scott Thompson said:

> The principalship, like any professional knowledge base, does not represent simply a body of subject content. It consists of knowledge and skills organized in a useful way preferably into work-relevant patterns that make expert knowledge functional. The professional preparation of principals, therefore, should instruct candidates broadly yet provide them—through classroom format, clinical practice, and field experience—with the practical knowledge and skills they need to address the daily challenges they will face. This approach does not preclude inquiry; rather it channels it in beneficial directions.

McCall (1994) championed the bringing together professors of educational administration and practicing school principals to develop the 21 domains into a meaningful publication. McCall believed the material offered was the type of practical guidance principals had been hoping for. He went so far as to call *Principals for Our Changing Schools* the watershed needed to embark on educational renewal. In it, what the principal has to know and do is embodied in the 21 domains. Eleven of the domains are process or skill oriented; 10 are more content focused; most synthesize knowledge and skill. The 21 domains are as follows:

I. Functional Domains

These domains focus on organizational processes and techniques by which the mission of the school is achieved. They provide for the educational program to be realized and allow the institution to function.

   A. Leadership

   B. Information Collection

   C. Problem Analysis

   D. Judgment

   E. Organizational Oversight

   F. Implementation

   G. Delegation

II. Programmatic Domains

These domains focus on the scope and framework of the educational program. They reflect the core technology of the schools, instruction, and the related supporting services, developmental activities, and resource base.

   A. Instruction and Learning Environment (instructional leadership)

   B. Curriculum Design

   C. Student Guidance and Development

   D. Staff Development

   E. Measurement and Evaluation

   F. Resource Allocation

III. Interpersonal Domains

These domains recognize the significance of interpersonal connections in schools. They acknowledge the critical value of human relationships to the satisfaction of personal and professional goals, and to the achievement of organizational purpose.

   A. Motivating Others

   B. Interpersonal Sensitivity

   C. Oral and Nonverbal Express

   D. Written Expression

IV. Contextual Domains

These domains reflect the world of ideas and forces within which the school operates. They explore the intellectual, ethical, cultural, economic, political, and government influences upon schools, including traditional and emerging perspectives.

  A. Philosophical and Cultural Values

  B. Legal and Regulatory Applications

  C. Policy and Political Influences

  D. Public Relations

THE SCHOOL LEARNING ORGANIZATION

Beginning in the early 1990s, the literature reflected a movement toward learning organizations and learning communities as a way of enhancing systemic reform of schools. The LEC utilized this literature as it proclaimed that schools must become self-renewing learning organizations (Keefe & Howard, 1997). Building upon the work of Peter Senge (1990), *The Fifth Discipline: The Art and Practice of the Learning Organization*, LEC presented a plan for *Redesigning Schools for the New Century: A Systems Approach* as reported by Keefe and Howard (1997). Senge (1990) said that learning organizations are places in which "people continually expand their capacity to create the results they truly desire, where new and expansive patterns of thinking are nurtured, where collective aspiration is set free, and where people are continually learning how to learn together." Learning organizations discover over time how to work together to create what the members mutually want to do (Keefe & Howard, 1997).

Learning organizations are distinguished by mastering five "learning disciplines" (Senge, 1990):

1. Shared Vision
2. Personal Mastery
3. Mental Models
4. Team Learning
5. Systems Thinking

Although mastered separately, together they build the learning organization.

Learning organizations focus on growth and continuous self-renewal with the principal having responsibility for building communities where people continue to expand their capabilities to shape their future (Ubben et al., 2001). Key to changing the learning environment in schools is the need to move away from a more traditional organization of schools as a business or a factory to one of a true learning organization.

Nevis, DiBella, and Gould (1995) defined organizational learning as "the capacity or processes within an organization to maintain or improve performance based on experience." Keefe and Howard (1997) stated, "successful learning organizations exhibit three characteristics that enable them to initiate and sustain improvement." These characteristics are:

1. *Well developed core competencies that serve as launch points for new products and services.* These competencies include such components as teacher selection and induction, staff development, instructional strategy, student's services, etc.
2. *Attitudes that support continuous improvement.* The cultural norms and expectations of the school must support a climate of student support and continuous improvement of the school's curriculum, instructional programs, communication structures, etc. The school climate must be positive, actively sustained, and risk-free.
3. *The capacity to redesign and renew.* Improvement is not an event but a process that must be continuously renewed and revitalized. Schools must have a design process in place that makes this possible.

It is the position of the LEC that the driver behind a school learning organization and school improvement is an SM/DT. This team should represent different stakeholders, and team members should be selected for their desire and commitment to improve the school. Schein (1993) presented several strategies that can help an SM/DT to become a learning team.

1. *Leaders must become learners.* Principals and other school leaders must overcome their school's cultural biases and learn about new ways and structures for doing things.

2. *The team must undergo its own learning process.* For the management/design team to function as a change agent in the school, it must develop its own cultural norms, trust level, and commitment to make innovative changes.

3. *The team must design the organization's learning process.* The first step in this is diagnosing the school's learning needs and forming task forces to deal with each of the major components of the emerging design.

4. *The task forces must develop detailed plans.* The plans should include specifications for new programs and strategies. The work of these task forces will become the Design Statement for the school.

5. *The management/design team must maintain communication and coordinate the work of task forces.* Systemic change requires attention to many elements of the organization at the same time and a studies attempt to move the process of change along in a coherent way.

THE PRINCIPAL AS INSTRUCTIONAL LEADER

Emerging from the MSP was the notion that the school principal should spend more time performing the role of "instructional leader." Since it was initially articulated, the concept of instructional leader has developed to the point where almost every textbook written about the school principal includes a substantial portion on the role of the principal as instructional leader. Looking at educational publishers' catalogs further illuminates the concept, as one can find many book titles that include the term "instructional leader."

The publication titled *Instructional Leader Handbook* (Keefe & Jenkins, 1991), published by the NASSP, was of major importance. It concluded that effective principals serve as instructional leaders in four ways: They possess a substantial knowledge base, and they plan, implement, and evaluate instructional programs collaboratively.

Kimbrough and Burkett (1990) concluded, after looking at research on the attainment of educational excellence, that the principal must be a strong instructional leader. They identified the instructional leadership tasks as follows:

• Leadership in reaching agreement on instructional goals.
• Leadership in decisions about the nature of curriculum content.

- Leadership in organizing curriculum experiences for learning.
- Leadership in improving the instructional program.
- Leadership in the evaluation of school performance.
- Maintaining an orderly climate.

Principals for Our Changing School: Knowledge and Skill Base (National Policy Board for Educational Administration, 1993) provides in Domain Eight, a definition of "Instruction and the Learning Environment," as:

Creating a school culture for learning; envisioning and enabling with others instructional and auxiliary programs for the improvement of teaching and learning recognizing the developmental needs of students; ensuring appropriate instructional methods; designing positive learning experiences; accommodating differences in cognition and achievement; mobilizing the participation of appropriate people and groups to develop these programs and to establish a positive learning environment.

Domain Eight in *Principals for Our Changing Schools: Knowledge and Skill Base* (National Policy Board for Educational Administration, 1993) provides a literature review indicating that research describes several characteristics of principals who are effective instructional leaders. First, they spend time differently than do less effective principals (Keefe, Clark, Nickerson, & Valentine, 1983; McCleary & Thomson, 1979; Pellicer, Anderson, Keefe, Kelley, & McCleary, 1988, 1990; Smith & Andrews, 1989). Second, their strong leadership has a positive effect on student achievement. Third, they generally perceive instructional leadership as a collegial process.

McCall (1994) further stated that effective principals perceive instructional leadership as a collegial process utilizing the following:

- hold teachers and students responsible to high expectations;
- spend a major portion of their day working with teachers to improve the educational program;
- work to identify and diagnose instructional problems; and
- become deeply involved in school culture and climate to influence student learning in positive ways.

In *Interstate School Leaders Consortium: Standards for School Leader* (1996), The Council of Chief State School Officers embraces the role of school administrators in the second standard as follows: "A school administrator is an educational leader who promotes the success of all students by advocating, nurturing, and sustaining a school culture and instructional program conducive to student learning and staff professional growth." *Breaking Ranks: Changing an American Institution* (1996), a report of the NASSP in partnership with the Carnegie Foundation for the advancement of teaching on the high school of the twenty-first century focused on leadership in chapter 13. The first four recommendations zeroed in on the principal as follows:

1. The principal will provide leadership in the high school community by building and maintaining a vision, direction, and focus for student learning.
2. Selection of high school principals will be based on qualities of leadership rooted in established knowledge and skills that result in dedication to good instructional practice and learning.
3. Current principals will build and refine the skills and knowledge required to lead and manage change.
4. The principal will foster an atmosphere that encourages teachers to take risks to meet the needs of students.

The document also supports the need for instructional leadership by stating,

An effective principal must inspire and lead by example. He or she should be a defender of academic integrity. Leadership qualities that distinguished some principals just a few years ago apply less and less as high schools move toward shared decision making and as site-based management and instructional leadership grow in importance.

In *High Schools of the Millennium*, a report of the American Youth Policy Forum (2000), the role of the high school principal was presented as follows:

the principal of a High School of the Millennium is the instructional leader of the school. He or she sets the tone for excellence and high achievement and creates an environment that encourages teachers and staff to constantly review and improve their instructional strategies to help students achieve. The principal aggressively seeks out the best information and practices in instructional strategies, especially strategies for students who are not performing at grade level, and ensures that staff and teachers know about and have access to such information, technical assistance, master teachers and coaches, and professional development.

Ubben and colleagues (2001) link the principal as builder of a learning community facilitating the learning process. Providing instructional leadership in the learning community as a facilitator of the instructional process is the responsibility of the principal. Ubben et al. report that many of the original models of instructional leadership were driven by an effective schools concept that placed the principal at the apex of learning. It is their contention, however, that effective instructional leadership requires a complex set of relationships between principals, their beliefs, and the surrounding environment of the school. Ubben and colleagues also present the idea that leadership in instructional and curricular endeavors is not just the responsibility of the principal alone, but that the principal solicits leadership from staff, students, and the community, as well.

Hoy and Hoy (2003) introduce the concept of the leadership role of the principal in developing a school climate that is conducive to providing the very best instructional practices. They contend that as the instructional leader, the principal is not alone in assuming responsibility for this task but leadership in instructional matters should be a collaborative effort between the principal and the teachers. It is the responsibility of the principal to develop a relationship with teachers that promotes a school climate where instructional leadership grows from teachers themselves. Hoy and Hoy (2003) believe that instructional leadership gets translated into action as follows:

- Academic excellence should be a strong motivating force in the school. Increasingly the research is affirming that a school's academic emphasis is critical to student achievement.
- Instructional excellence and continuous improvement are ongoing and cooperative activities by instructional leaders and teachers.

- Teachers are at the center of the instructional improvement; in the end, only the teachers themselves can change and improve their educational practice in the classroom.
- Principals must provide constructive support and obtain the resources and materials necessary for teachers to be successful in the classroom.
- Principals should be intellectual leaders who keep abreast of the latest developments in teaching, learning, motivation, classroom management, and assessment.
- The principal should take the lead in recognizing and celebrating academic excellence among students and teachers because such activities reinforce a vision and culture of academic excellence.

Daresh (2002) indicated that newer emerging leadership perspectives in school administration have been directed toward the theme of an administrator as instructional leader. Daresh further stated that most of the early attempts to define leadership behavior were in very narrow terms. He contends that we now recognize that individuals other than the school principal may be involved in instructional leadership behaviors, and that we have increasingly realized that instructional leadership can take forms that go well beyond direct intervention in classroom activities. To support this view, Daresh quotes a definition of instructional leadership by Ching-Jen Liu (1984) : "Instructional Leadership consists of direct or indirect behaviors that significantly affect teacher instruction and, as a result, student learning." Building on the concepts of direct and indirect behaviors, Daresh explains direct leadership activities as staff development and teacher evaluation and supervision. Indirect leadership is described as instructional facilitation, resource acquisition and building maintenance, and student problem recognition.

After reviewing a number of documents, including many of those listed previously, McEwan (2003) believed that three major themes regarding the school principal emerged:

1. The focus of the principalship must be shifted from management to instructional leadership.
2. Instructional leadership is essential to developing and sustaining excellent schools.
3. There is a shortage of trained administrators who are capable of handling the demands of instructional leadership.

In *Seven Steps to Effective Instructional Leadership*, McEwan reviewed the literature on the instructional leader and presented the following seven steps to effective leadership:

1. Establish, implement, and achieve academic standards.
2. Be an instructional resource for your staff.
3. Create a school culture and climate conducive to learning.
4. Communicate the vision and mission of your school.
5. Set high expectations for your staff and yourself.
6. Develop teacher leaders.
7. Develop and maintain positive relationships with students, staff, and parents.

THE TRANSFORMATIONAL LEADER

Burns (1978) presented two differing leadership styles when he identified *transactional* and *transformational* leadership. Burns felt they represent completely different styles and that they are at opposite ends of a continuum. The transactional leader works from a power base of rewards and punishments seeking to gain the cooperation of followers on an "exchange" basis. Leadership is seen as a function or organizational position. A transactional principal then focuses on tightly coupled objectives, curriculum, teaching strategies, and evaluation. Teachers are viewed as "workers in the field," with administration determining not only the "what" but also the "how." According to Burns, a transformational leader inspires others toward collaboration and interdependence as they work toward a purpose to which they are deeply committed.

Transactional leadership is based on influence and is accomplished when leaders "delegate and surrender power over people and events in order to achieve power over accomplishments and goal achievement." Burns (1978) proposed that transformational leadership is relational, and it deals with producing real change. He further explains: "Transformational leadership occurs when one or more persons engage with others in such a way that leaders and followers raise one another to higher levels of motivation and morality." Shriberg, Shriberg, and Lloyd (2002) believe that transformational leadership has a moral dimension and that it is a relationship between leaders and followers in which both are elevated to more principled levels of judgment. It is about power "to" rather than power "over."

Bass (1985) contends that leaders must manage before they can lead. The leader must first be concerned with understanding subordinates' needs, providing them with appropriate rewards for their contributions, and helping them clarify the connection between their goals and those of the organization. According to Bass, true leaders inspire others to greater values awareness, encourage their commitment to the goals of the organization, or foster their personal or professional growth, and it is during this process that the leader becomes transformational.

Sergiovanni's (1984) model of the effective instructional leader presents a continuum of leadership skills by dividing them into lower level and higher level skills. At the lowest level are the technical, human, and educational skills, which, according to Sergiovanni are the most basic skills for determing competence as a leader. A school principal would need to master these skills for good management and to be deemed as competent. Before a school principal is considered to be effective or transformational they must exhibit the two highest skills, symbolic and cultural.

Foster (1984) suggests that transformational leadership results from "mutual negotiations and shared leadership roles." He believes that "leadership cannot occur without followership and many times the two are exchangeable. That is, leaders normally have to negotiate visions and ideas with potential followers, who may in turn become leaders themselves, renegotiating the particular agenda."

The ERIC Clearinghouse on Educational Management (1993), in its review of the literature on change, points out that when the principal plays a transformational role, teachers blossom as instructional leaders because the principal encourages and elicits these talents. A principal strives toward these ends by promoting staff ownership of change, developing a leadership team, managing decision making in group settings, and building community support for the school.

Breaking Ranks (NASSP, 1996) presents the principal as the person in a pivotal position to bring about successful school reform. It describes the transformational leader as the "keeper of the dream."

SUMMARY

A lot has transpired since the seminal work of J. Lloyd Trump and others to bring about comprehensive school renewal with the implementation of the MSP. This chapter has attempted to look at the concept of the SMT within the MSP and how it has been modified and yet retained much of the original thinking behind the model, with the school principal in the key leadership role as instructional leader. We have looked at how the role of the principal has been viewed and changed, especially since the MSP. Research on the effectiveness of the principal and identification of various special projects to identify the tasks and skills required by principals were presented to provide a context for the changing role of the principal. We took a look at the school as a learning organization and how it is consistent with the LEC focus on systemic renewal.

Emanating from the MSP, the concept of the school principal as instructional leader emerged, and we reviewed some literature related to the instructional leader. Lastly, we took a look at the research and literature on transformational leadership.

Interestingly, much of what was originally presented in the MSP in regard to the role of the principal and the SMT has remained, except in a slightly different form. The idea that the school principal should not be burdened with "administravia" and should spend more time being an instructional leader has become a major focus of educational professionals today. The SMT has undergone several revisions moving to a leadership team and now embracing the concept of a learning organization. However, the idea of a team has been retained in all of these transformations but it has been opened up to include many more individuals. The idea of a "design team" working together as a learning organization is one of the central components for school renewal and the LEC today.

The changing role of the school principal began with the MSP, where the idea of the school principal spending a greater amount of time as the instructional leader has not only remained today but also has been strengthened by research and the literature supporting the need for strong instructional leadership for successful schools. The numbers of books with the title "instructional leadership" or that include chapter(s) on instructional leadership provide evidence of this lasting effect from the MSP.

Leadership in the twenty-first century has brought forth new paradigms, including the servant leadership paradigm of Robert Greenleaf, the concept of transformational leadership championed by James Mac-Gregor Burns, and critical transformational theory from the Brazilian educator Paulo Freire. The transformational leader is in concert with the instructional leader and learning organizations. It can be said that all three have strong roots in the MSP of the National Association of School Principals.

Just as important as the impact of ideas regarding the role of the principal and the SMT, is the fact that many of the individuals associated with the MSP have continued to be actively involved in the profession, the NASSP, and the LEC. Major reports and projects—such as the Carnegie Foundation's *Turning Points* (1989), the National Policy Board's report titled *Principals for Our Changing Schools: Knowledge and Skill Base* (1993), the NASSP's *Breaking Ranks* (1996), and the Council of Chief State School Officers' *Interstate School Leaders Licensure Consortium: Standards for School Leaders* (1996)—were influenced by the MSP, and many of the individuals involved with MSP and the LEC served on commissions that developed these reports.

CHAPTER 3

Teacher Role and Advisement

John M. Jenkins

Webster's New Collegiate Dictionary defines a profession as a condition when "the whole body of a person is engaged in a calling," and a professional as a person "characterized by or conforming to the technical standards of a profession." One of the major tenets of the MSP was the professionalization of the role of the teacher. The model was committed to finding time for teachers to work on curriculum and evaluation and to perform a number of professional tasks that teachers only have limited time to do in conventional schools. These tasks included developing instructional materials, planning curriculum, improving student assessment, advising students, and meeting with parents. In conventional schools, such tasks are overshadowed by a variety of nonprofessional duties including campus supervision, clerical responsibilities, distribution of books and materials, and supervising students working alone or in small groups.

The numerous nonprofessional duties assigned to teachers keep them from devoting appropriate time to tasks specifically related to improving student learning. In the medical profession, doctors rarely, if ever, carry bedpans. They generally don't take temperatures or blood pressure, or administer injections. These tasks are handled by others who have lesser training yet are competent to do the job. The MSP called for the implementation of a differentiated staffing model whereby the adult–student ratio would be decreased and the teacher–student ratio increased. Principals in the model schools traded teaching positions for paraprofessional positions, usually at a rate of three to one.

There were three categories of paraprofessionals: instructional, clerical, and general, each with specific responsibilities. Because instructional aides worked directly with students as they completed assigned work on their own or with small groups of students, they were required to have two years of college or the equivalent in the assigned subject area. Clerical aides typed, duplicated, and distributed materials. They also helped complete much of the paperwork often done by teachers, such as grade recording and tracking attendance. General aides supervised the cafeteria, halls, and bus loading and unloading. No specific skills were needed except being able to relate well to students and having good character. The standard was 20 hours per week, times the number of teachers in the school, for *instructional assistants*, 10 hours per week, times the number of teachers, for *clerical aides*, and five hours per week, times the number of teachers, for *general aides.*

Differentiated staffing existed, however, as part of an array of school components and not in isolation. Among the components were such innovative practices as the continuous progress sequencing of curriculum, team teaching, advisement, flexible scheduling, and a diagnostic-prescriptive approach to personalized learning. The MSP prescribed changes in many aspects of the school simultaneously, on the premise that change in one area impacted change in other areas. One might conclude that the model seemed to foreshadow the notion of Senge's systemic reform that would come later in the twentieth century.

In the early 1970s the conditions for differential staffing were much more efficacious because there was a surplus of teachers. Certified teachers who were not successful in getting hired often accepted positions as instructional assistants in the hope that later they could obtain a teaching position. This was especially true of first-year teachers who viewed the opportunity to serve as an instructional assistant as an appropriate induction into the culture of teaching. But the external environment changed, and teacher organizations began to see the trading of teaching units for aides as not in the best interest of the profession. A reduction in the number of assistants made it difficult for teachers to do all of the professional planning associated with the MSP. Currently, however, with the teaching profession experiencing a shortage of teachers, it is possible that some form of differentiated staffing might be one way to address the problem. It may appear reasonable to consider non-certified personnel with baccalaureate degrees in the role of *instructional assistants* working directly with students under the supervision of certified teachers. Rather than filling teaching positions with non-certified personnel, the same funds could be used to employ various levels of paraprofessionals to enable certified teachers to use their school time more professionally.

The present No Child Left Behind Act, passed by the U.S. Congress in January 2002, requires that teacher aides who work directly with students hold an associate of arts degree and/or pass a state or local proficiency examination. Thus, there appears at the national level recognition that persons working directly with students in the schools must meet certain standards. Currently, about 642,000 aides work in the public schools, with titles varying from school to school: paraprofessionals, instructional aides, educational assistants, or simply "paras" (Labbe, 2002).

While the new legislation addresses the need for qualified teacher aides, it fails to acknowledge other tasks within a school that infringe on a teacher's professional time. The differential staffing model of the MSP might appropriately serve as a point of departure for giving teachers the kinds of assistance that would enable them to exercise true professional leadership in meeting the academic needs of all students.

PERSONALIZING INSTRUCTION

Personalized instruction was a major goal of the MSP and the major thrust of the LECI for school improvement and reform. LECI identifies six basic elements of personalized instruction to guide educators in designing and implementing programs for student success:

1. a dual teacher role of coach and adviser,
2. the diagnosis of relevant student learning characteristics,
3. a collegial school environment,
4. an interactive learning environment,
5. flexible scheduling and pacing, and
6. authentic assessment. (Keefe & Jenkins, 2000)

These features distinguish the culture and context of personalized learning. Of the six elements, the teacher role is ostensibly the key to the development and implementation of a personalized system of instruction. What a teacher does daily, and over time, establishes a framework for student success. It is the classroom teacher who understands what is best for individual students and what is possible within the context of district and state policies. Personalized instruction requires that teachers assume the dual role of subject-matter coach and teacher-adviser to a finite number of students.

TEACHER AS COACH

Similar to athletic coaches, teachers move from the front of a group of students to the side of individual students or small groups of students. They offer the same kind of instruction, demonstration, practice, and feedback to their students as do athletic coaches. As such, teachers recognize that attempting to serve as a repository of knowledge in any subject is futile, given the nature of the knowledge explosion over the past several decades. "Covering" subject matter or the textbook seems antithetical to the contingencies of today's ethos. The teacher-coach is a facilitator of learning, a "learning guide" who leads students to appropriate learning resources. He or she prepares instructional objectives, analyzes the strengths and weaknesses of individual students in relation to the objectives, and investigates and makes available a wide range of activities and resources that will facilitate student success.

Joyce and Showers (1982) identify five major functions of coaching. Coaching makes provision for:

1. Companionship—interchange with another human being over a difficult process;
2. Technical feedback—perfecting skills, polishing them, and working through problem areas;
3. Analysis of application—deciding when to use a particular strategy or tactic;
4. Adaptation to students—adjusting the approach to fit the needs, skill level, and backgrounds of particular students; and
5. Personal facilitation—helping students feel good about their efforts as they practice new skills.

In *The Paideia Proposal,* Mortimer Adler (1982) identifies learning by discovery as the quintessential element in creating a community of learning. In Adler's estimation, only geniuses are able to discover unaided. For most students, discovery must be aided. Coaching, therefore, assumes prominence as one of the three key approaches to teaching and learning. Adler claims, "the absence of . . . individualized coaching in our schools explains why most of the students cannot read well, write well, speak well, listen well, or perform well any of the basic intellectual operations." David Perkins (1992) has revisited the three Paideia approaches in an approach he calls Theory One. He encourages good didactic instruction when appropriate, coaching for skills training, practice, and feedback, and Socratic seminars for open-ended, thoughtful discussions. Coaching or guided practice is also a key component of several advanced teaching strategies, namely, reciprocal teaching, cognitive apprenticeships, and topic study (also known as storyline).

TEACHER AS ADVISER

The concept of the teacher as adviser to a small number of students was one of the most popular elements of the MSP, as judged by its sustaining influence in middle and high schools over the past 30 years and its widespread adoption at both levels. It was reasoned that the guidance counselor–student ratio of 300 or more to 1 far exceeded the ability of one counselor to know his/her counselees well enough to personalize the educational process. By having teachers and administrators serving as advisers to a smaller number, usually 25 or less to 1, students could be known as "total human beings" educationally. The professional counselors could then be freed to utilize their special preparation to work with students needing special assistance, to provide in-depth career counseling, to help students with college admissions, and to interpret test results to groups and individuals.

Educators with experience in private education know that frequently the role of the teacher is extended to include the advisement and guidance of students during and beyond the regular school day. Teachers are expected to be more than just an "expert" in a given field of knowledge.

They are expected to relate well to their students and to serve as role model, mentor, and sometimes confidant.

The first formal public school advisement program on record was found at the New Trier High School in Winnetka, Illinois in 1924. Named the Adviser-Personnel Plan, it was "designed to provide educational, vocational, social, moral, and ethical guidance and counsel to all students in the school" (Clerk, 1928, p. 1). Teacher-advisers were assigned by grade levels and remained with their respective advisees throughout their high school careers.

At New Trier, the teacher-advisers were expected to function as a teacher and friend to their advisees. Visits to the homes of each advisee were completed by Thanksgiving. The personal nature of the New Trier system is captured in the following description in the Adviser-Personnel Plan, "The adviser is expected to study each one of the advisees with the greatest care and sympathy with a view to understanding him thoroughly and gaining his confidence" (Clerk, 1928, p. 13). Teacher-advisers at New Trier also served as the first line of referral in the school's discipline procedures. Since they knew the referred student best, it was surmised that they were in the most efficacious position to help resolve the problem.

An adviser period, similar to homeroom, was scheduled each day for one half hour. Advisers conducted group activities from content outlines developed for each grade level and met with individual advisees either during the period or after school. Later, in 1956, as the school population grew, advisory groupings combated the anonymity often accompanying bigness and offered the students "a home away from home." Advisers were given the additional responsibility of identifying students with serious emotional problems and referring those students to the school counselors. A clear connection was established between advisement and the overall school guidance program.

In 1983, Keefe identified overall guidance activities as either administrative or clinical depending on the purpose. He defined the major guidance services as career information, instructional units, registration and placement, records maintenance, testing, counseling, and referral. His guidance continuum ranges from instructional information at one end to therapy at the other.

In Keefe's description, advisement focuses on the instructional aspects cutting across several of the guidance functions that do not require specialized training. He sees advisers as assisting with registration and scheduling, giving information regarding career and college options, offering guidance on school-related problems, monitoring advisees' academic progress, and interacting with classroom teachers in an endeavor to provide salient information to improve instruction for individual advisees.

Four major areas seem to encompass the activities of the teacher-as-adviser: adviser-advisee relationships, adviser-staff interactions, adviser-parent contacts, and advisory group activities. Of the four areas, the adviser-advisee relationship is indispensable to personalizing instruction. By conducting frequent individual conferences, the teacher-adviser comes to know the advisee well and obtains information that can affect his/her academic performance in the school. The individual conferences focus on monitoring the advisee's academic progress, reviewing and sometimes interpreting test scores, helping advisees with course registration and with long-range academic plans, and getting to know the advisees' interests, hobbies, and future plans. Teacher-advisers may even assist advisees with the development of a postgraduate plan, articulating the student's purpose beyond obtaining a high school diploma.

The teacher-adviser is a diagnostician who communicates salient information about individual advisees to appropriate teachers. When a student fails to progress satisfactorily in a given subject area, often it is the teacher-adviser, working with the classroom teacher, who helps ameliorate the problem. He or she helps classroom teachers find successful ways to help students learn. In schools that administer some form of learning style instrument, the teacher-advisers may review an advisee's profile and map appropriate study skills to take advantage of his or her strengths. When schools include cognitive skills in the diagnosis, the adviser may recommend augmentation strategies or refer the advisee to a school counselor or a cognitive resource teacher, if the school has such a person.

Advisers also communicate with advisees' parents, keeping them informed regarding academic progress and enlisting their help in gaining information that could have an impact on teaching an advisee differently. They may meet with an advisee's parents during the course selection and registration period.

Advisory group activities focus on the guidance curriculum, informing students about careers, colleges and universities, testing options, academic credentials, study skills, and promotion and graduation requirements. Many middle schools and some high schools schedule advisory group activities on a regular basis. School counselors or advisement coordinators frequently develop lesson plans for advisory group activities to provide program continuity and to help busy teacher-advisers.

The nub of advisement is "getting to know students well enough to know what is best for him or her" (Powell, Farrar, & Cohen, 1985). *Breaking Ranks: Changing an American Institution*, a report of the NASSP on the high school of the twenty-first century, contains the recommendation that "Every high school student will have a personal adult advocate to help him or her personalize the educational experience" (NASSP, 1996, p. 29).

TEACHER AS LEADER

Ideally, teachers in the MSP worked directly with students only 20 hours per week. The other 20 hours were devoted to planning instruction, evaluating student progress, developing curriculum materials, analyzing needs, and advising students. This arrangement was achieved by organizing the teaching faculty in teams with differential responsibilities. A "master" teacher led each team. Teams were often given a great deal of latitude for making decisions. Much interaction occurred among team members and across team arrangements throughout the school.

The LEC recommends extending the concept of teaming to encompass the entire school. This arrangement facilitates a collegial environment where teachers, administrators, and students engage in frequent interaction directed toward school improvement. When schools become places in which teachers work together to achieve desirable results, a learning organization begins to take shape where each teacher's input is elicited and valued. As learning organizations, schools become environments where teachers continually learn. In essence they become "communities of learning" for teachers and students.

Teachers, in a community of learners, model for students their own enthusiasm for learning as they seek to improve their ability to facilitate student learning more effectively. As school populations become increasingly diverse, teachers must learn how to deal effectively with all types of students. Simply focusing on teaching successfully those students perceived to be the most capable is not sufficient. If all students are to be served, it is incumbent upon teachers in the twenty-first century to expand their knowledge base in order to engage all students effectively.

Three aspects of instruction relate directly to its personalization: (a) diagnosing and accommodating learning style differences, (b) multiple intelligences, and (c) authentic forms of pedagogy. *Learning style* addresses how students learn and how they like to learn. *Multiple intelligences* focus on how cultures and disciplines shape potential. *Authentic forms of pedagogy* connect classroom learning and the world beyond the classroom. In each case, a considerable knowledge base exists for teachers to comprehend. All three offer direction for helping students master difficult content and skills. The following statement from Linda Darling-Hammond (1997) captures this role of teachers as "lifelong" learners:

> A more complex, knowledge-based and multi-cultural society creates new expectations for teaching. To help diverse learners master more challenging content, teachers must go far beyond dispensing information, giving a test, and giving a grade. They must themselves know their subject areas deeply, and they must understand how students think, if they are to create experiences that actually work to produce learning. (p. 194)

THE FINDINGS

The director of the MSP, J. Lloyd Trump, cited the lack of empirical evidence to support many of the accomplishments over the five-year duration of the project. Even though most of the innovative strategies were not new and had their origins in previous private and public school practice, there was little empirically derived evidence to advocate their adoption by nonparticipating middle and high schools. Although the project conducted a number of studies and participating schools did likewise, the resulting data did not provide a template for school improvement. Subsequent studies conducted after the project ended began to show the worth of some of the innovations, especially the value of advisement.

A five-year evaluation of the Teachers-as-Advisors Program in Florida showed a clear decrease in the number of dropouts in high schools where advisement programs were instituted (Florida Department of Education, 1991). Improvements in daily attendance were found in over half of 122 high schools, and improved attendance is a correlate of improved academic performance (Florida Department of Education, 1990). At both the middle and high school levels, fewer disciplinary referrals were recorded in schools with advisement programs. Even fewer disciplinary referrals were found in schools that had established advisement programs when compared with schools that were just undertaking a program (Florida Department of Education, 1991).

In *Turning Points: Preparing American Youth for the 21st Century* (Carnegie Council on Adolescent Development Task Force, 1990), it was observed that

> the effect of the advisory system appears to be to reduce alienation of students and to provide each adolescent with the support of a caring adult who knows the student well. That bond can make the student's engagement and interest in learning a reality.

Advisement has also been a part of the CES where it has emerged as an important way to work toward making a student's education more personal (Cushman, 1990). Advisement theory and practice was seen as a major combatant of the impersonal nature of "the shopping mall high school" as reported in one of the triumvirate of books spawned by the NASSP Study of High Schools that presaged the establishment of the Coalition (Powell et al., 1985).

The teacher-as-coach or guide follows a familiar model in the arts and athletics. It is a model that has persisted through the twentieth century and beyond, involving students practicing a target behavior under the watchful eye of a teacher-coach. By carefully observing what a student does, the teacher-coach suggests steps to improve. Further practice is then engaged. The practice-observation-feedback process continues until the student is able to perform the behavior independently. In personalized approaches to instruction, teachers are cognizant of student strengths and shortcomings and offer specific recommendations for further learning and improvement.

Sylvia Farnham-Diggory (1994) contends that there are only four basic teaching methods: (a) talking (lecturing, questioning); (b) displaying (modeling, demonstrating); (c) coaching (cuing, guiding); and (d) arranging the learning environment. Coaching and arranging the learning environment are often interrelated. Coaching is more successful if the learning environment is friendly, supportive, resource-rich, and interactive. Like advisement, coaching is a major feature of the CES. It is a way for students to "gain skills through critiqued experience" (Sizer, 1984).

The value of coaching can also be found in *Breaking Ranks,* as captured in the following recommendation: "Teachers will be adept at acting as coaches and facilitators of learning to promote more active involvement of students in their own learning" (NASSP, 1996, p. 21). The narrative expanding this recommendation describes the connection between coaching and engaged learning:

> Coaching involves a kind of teaching that creates active learners. The student investigates multiple approaches to solving a math problem or expounds on the meaning of the novel or conducts the physics experiment. But the teacher-coach remains nearby—observing, asking questions, prodding the student to reflect on the product of his or her efforts. The student's response or performance—the learning experience—becomes the subject of the coaching. (p. 23)

In an endeavor to add to teacher professionalism, the National Policy Board for Professional Teaching Standards has established national standards in over 30 certificate fields. Teachers desirous of receiving national certification in a given discipline must meet the standards in a variety of ways. While the standards may vary from discipline to discipline, they are influenced by five core propositions that seem to summarize the reshaping of new roles for public school teachers:

- Teachers are committed to students and their learning.
- Teachers know the subjects they teach and how to teach those subjects to students.

- Teachers are responsible for managing and monitoring student learning.
- Teachers think systematically about their practice and learn from experience.
- Teachers are members of learning communities.

Given the paucity of empirical evidence to support these new roles for teachers, it may appear difficult to offer a cogent argument for any of them. Their worth, however, may reside in the observations of literally thousands of involved teachers. With the advent of two developments—(a) qualitative research methodology, and (b) the rediscovery of the teacher-as-researcher, also known as action research—hard evidence to validate each of the roles may be forthcoming. Each of these new roles for teachers is fertile ground for the researcher and the practitioner alike.

CHAPTER 4

Student Role: Large Group, Small Group, and Independent Study

Robert E. Lowery and John M. Jenkins

The role of the students in any school setting seems twofold: (1) to acquire the knowledge, skills, and attitudes needed to take their place in a rapidly changing society, and (2) to discover and develop their unique talents so as to participate creatively in the society, which has given them life. How students accomplish these ends really depends on the kind of school they attend and the expectations the school personnel hold for each student. In too many instances, educators take pride in the accomplishments of a few students while losing sight of the greater challenge of success for all.

Forty years ago, the Model Schools Project (MSP) was initiated, which incorporated the concept of involving students in a more personalized role in their educational endeavors. Independent study, or IS, as it was labeled, became the main focus of a student's daily routine, with large group (LG) motivational presentations and small group (SG) interactive seminars providing a supporting role.

The MSP's director, Dr. J. Lloyd Trump, liked to quip that independent study was "the activities students engage in when the teacher stops talking." Obviously, Dr. Trump knew that independent study was much more encompassing and required the preparation of materials designed to engage the student's interest and to move him/her along a continuum of achievement in each subject area, but overstated his case in order to make a point. He believed that real learning is an active, not a passive, process. It engages students in their own education and challenges them to advance as far as their time, talent, and motivation permit.

The framework for achieving this ideal was the continuous monitoring of each student's academic progress using the procedures of *diagnosis*, *prescription*, *implementation*, and *evaluation* (DPIE) based on knowing the student as a unique person. Most traditional schools focus on the classroom or group and deliver similar instruction to all the students. Adjustments for background knowledge, learning style, or interest are often overlooked in order to cover the required curriculum efficiently.

In the MSP, curriculum was defined in terms of essential, desirable, and advanced content in each of eight or nine subject areas. These areas included language arts, social studies, mathematics, science, other cultures, practical arts, fine arts, health, and fitness and recreation, as well as religion in parochial schools. Scopes and sequences or course descriptions were developed for each of the subjects, to enable students to begin the study of a subject commensurate with what they knew and to advance accordingly. Usually, learning guides were prepared by teachers to be consistent with the course descriptions and to lead students to various materials and activities to help them achieve designated objectives.

Students were scheduled into large group presentation sessions of 100 or more students in each subject area every two weeks. The presentations typically drew their content from the current scene to add an aura of reality to what students did in their independent study. Since the students who listened to the motivational presentations would be at various stages in their independent study, the presentations were not related directly to what the students were doing at any particular moment. Rather, they represented a generalized stimulation to all students to open their minds to greater potential in the subjects, to reveal career opportunities and other practical considerations, or to otherwise make the study more meaningful (Trump, 1969). The teacher-planned large group presentations were primarily motivational in nature; but they also were informational, providing facts and ideas not readily available to students, and directional, suggesting or assigning independent activities for further study (Georgiades, 1978). In some of the model schools, it was common practice for the students to become involved as presenters in large group sessions. This participation offered students in-depth opportunities in preparing the materials that would be used in their presentations.

Large group presentations were followed by small group reaction or clarification sessions with about 15 students. Small groups guided by a teacher enabled the students to ask questions about what they had experienced in the large groups. The size of the group also encouraged more student interaction.

Independent study, the third component of the MSP triad, had been a part of formal schooling for decades. Study halls, supervised study in regular classrooms, going to the library, and even homework meet the criteria for independent study. The difference between previous manifestations and the Model Schools Project approach was how independent study was implemented. First the MSP settings varied—a minimum of three venues was considered: the school, the home, and the community. Second, the emphasis in the MSP was on the student's role in learning. Students were asked to accept much of the responsibility for selecting materials from among an array of resources in completing their work. In some cases, they were asked to define their own areas of study beyond what was required. The model listed five goals for independent study as follows:

1. to gain self direction and self-control,
2. to use a variety of materials,
3. to work with a variety of human resources,
4. to individualize learning, and
5. to promote self-evaluation.

INTEGRATING LARGE GROUP, SMALL GROUP, AND INDEPENDENT STUDY

The Model Schools Project hoped to integrate LG, SG, and IS strategies into the instructional program to be responsive to the needs of students. In one school all students regularly participated in motivational large group presentations in each of the eight or nine content areas, even when they were not enrolled in a specific subject area for credit. The large group presentations were conducted throughout the school year and incorporated lectures, panel discussions, demonstrations, performances, and media presentations. Some were student-prepared and presented for credit in topics such as existentialism in literature, the uses of science, and dance as an art form.

Students also participated in small group discussions on the topics presented in the large groups or on some other topics suggested by current events related to the area of learning. The key components for the students were communication and interaction. There were also special seminars related to required or elective classes. In some cases, students would sign up for a content-oriented discussion when they had completed the work in a curriculum unit. At times, students would also form an independent seminar with a teacher to explore advanced topics in a specific field. The key elements for students in these sessions were, again, communication and interaction.

Students spent much of their time on independent study, working by themselves or with others. Their progress was carefully monitored by a teacher and by a teacher-adviser. The subject area content was the same as in a traditional school, but the students worked at their own pace and level of difficulty. All independent study curricula were organized into learning units or "learning guides"—a set of directions indicating the main idea, course objectives, and alternative learning activities and sometimes the evaluation options to establish goals and plan programs for the students. Students worked with teachers serving as subject consultants in each subject area when they needed special help or wished to arrange to explore a topic in greater depth.

Students were scheduled at all times but had a variety of choices within the program.

About 90% of the students were scheduled for independent study. The other 10% had a more structured schedule. As the students in a structured schedule demonstrated a willingness and a maturity level sufficient to handle independent study, they were offered the opportunity for independent study. Usually these students experienced a gradual transition from total structure to increasingly more independent study.

The student's schedule was arranged in cooperation with a teacher-adviser who was empowered to place students into one or more resource centers during the school day. Subject area spaces contained resource centers where students received learning guides and other materials to complete their work. In one school, facilities were constructed to house the Model Schools Project. In most, however, traditional facilities were modified to accommodate large group, small group, and independent study.

Thus, the student role in the MSP involved (1) setting goals with their teacher-adviser; (2) participating in large groups, small groups, and seminars; (3) deciding whether to be involved in several subjects or to concentrate on one or two for a limited time; (4) deciding whether to graduate early or not and organizing their program accordingly; and (5) the chance to be more mature and self-directed in the entire high school experience.

A DECADE OR TWO LATER

As the schools in the Model Schools Project evolved, changes were inevitable. A small group of schools, mostly on the west coast of the United States and Canada, formed the Learning Environments Consortium (LEC) in an endeavor to maintain and further develop aspects of the Model Schools Project. In some cases, major changes were made, but the underlying tenets remained, namely, (1) the uniqueness of the individual student, (2) developing student responsibility and self-direction, and (3) the willingness to change direction when necessary and appropriate.

Keefe's (1989) expanded DPIE model was adopted by LEC. He identified three specific components under each of the major headings of diagnosis, prescription, implementation, and evaluation. For example, diagnosis included a student's learning history, developmental level, and learning style. The learning style component, vestigial in the Model Schools Project, became more comprehensive in scope. Assessment instruments had been developed in the 1970s and later to provide teachers and teacher-advisers with data about how students learn and how they like to learn. These data could become part of a student profile, which was available to adjust instruction to individual student preferences and needs. Subsequent developments in cognitive science provided educators with an even deeper understanding of how individual students processed information. Flavell and Wellman (1977), for example, described four levels of mental activity beginning with processes that are hardwired and ending with metacognitive skills whereby students have a conscious awareness of themselves as problem solvers. Diagnosing a student's placement on one of the four levels further enables a teacher to develop appropriate instructional environments.

Large group motivational sessions were never really implemented in accordance with the model's recommendations by very many of the schools in the project. Most schools eschewed the motivational large groups and focused mainly on small group seminars, help sessions, and independent study. When implemented, most large groups were instructional in nature, presenting information to students as a means of acquiring subject matter content. The motivational aspect of typical large group presentations became sporadic and was reserved for special events and guest speakers.

Since the small group concept was included in the Model Schools Project for clarification and reaction to the large group motivational session, small groups also changed over time. Seminars that focused on specific content and help sessions for students with special needs became more numerous. Table 4.1, containing the course outline for English 10 at Bishop Carroll High School, Calgary, Alberta (one of the original MSP schools, and still successfully operating), illustrates the transition in utilizing small groups.

Independent study based on continuous progress scheduling, course outlines, and learning guides is still being used in several high schools. Currently, the Canadian Coalition for Self-Directed Learning supports this approach. It is found in some form in all seven of the Coalition's participating secondary schools. The learning guides are less linear than the guides found in the original Model Schools Project. While the guides still encourage self-pacing on the part of the student, the addition of various pathways to common ends requires students to make more choices. One of the Coalition schools, Thomas Haney Secondary Centre, prefers the description "supported independent study." Students are not left to work alone; they have the support of teachers and teacher-advisers in making choices and completing the learning guides. At Haney, independent learning involves the students in large group presentations, seminar groups, and one-to-one consultation, all in the context of regular student and teacher communications. Cross-curricular programs enable students to negotiate credit for completing some learning guides in more than one subject area.

Table 4.1. English 10-1 Course Outline

Unit Value	Unit Topic/Title	Weighting	Comment
1	Orientation		
1	Critical Responses		
2	Autobiography	10%	All Grade 10 Students September 9 to October 4
3	Poetry	15%	This compulsory seminar is held every Thursday at 10:00 a.m. in Room 357. Sign-up is required.
3	Short Story	15%	This compulsory seminar is held every Tuesday at 1:00 p.m. in Room 357. Sign-up is required.

The following program combines both small group seminars and online learning units to maximize continuous progress and independent study.

Example of Seminar Activities (Poetry)

A. **Pre-Seminar Activities:** You must read through and familiarize yourself with the poetry terminology in this learning guide before you attend the seminar.

B. In the seminar, you will be asked to work in small groups of 3 or 4; in your groups you will have the opportunity to demonstrate your understanding of the poetic devices and also your creativity. At the end of the seminar, groups will share their efforts. The group process and your contributions to the group will be evaluated during this seminar; it is advisable that you come to the seminar prepared to be an effective group member. Be sure to consider the **rubric** that will be used for **evaluation purposes**.

You will review how to write a critical response on poetry. The review will involve direct teaching and small group activities.

At the end of the seminar, you will be given the designated poetry text and be asked to prepare a specific poem for evaluation (Critical Response). Additional resources will also be provided.

C. Following the seminar and after you have written your practice critical response; bring it to any English teacher in Humanities to check to see if you are on the right track.

D. Students will submit the following work **within two weeks** after the seminar:

- Practice critical response
- A brief biography (maximum 300 words) on the poet studied
- A list of three websites used to conduct your research
- An evaluation of these websites
- Another poem by this poet
- A formulated thesis statement for your chosen poem
- Your own poem on the seminar topic
- A critical response on your own poem

E. Write the Poetry Test in the Testing Center after attending the seminar. The test will comprise two parts: a reading comprehension (multiple choice) and a critical response on a sight (that means one you have not seen previously) poem.

---

* Note: Underlining added.

CURRENT APPROACHES TO PERSONALIZED INSTRUCTION

The work of the Model Schools Project and the initial extensions of that effort by the Learning Environments Consortium created a prologue for current initiatives in personalized learning. Obviously, educators know much more today about teaching and learning than they did 40 years ago. While some of these approaches still focus on individualized instruction and self-pacing, not all do. Personalized instruction builds on the DPIE model but looks at a variety of ways to deal with individual students. Interestingly, even direct instruction can be a form of personalized instruction for some students.

In 2000, Keefe and Jenkins identified 20 different approaches to personalized instruction. They rated each of these 20 approaches on the degree of interaction and thoughtfulness encouraged in students. At the lowest end of this two-dimensional matrix were individualized instruction, mastery learning, and direct instruction. At the highest end were cognitive apprenticeships, cooperative learning, guided practice, and topic study (sometimes called storyline).

For each of the 20 strategies, student roles differ. For example, students are much less active when experiencing direct instruction than they are in topic study. The latter, developed in Scotland, identifies a topic or problem to be investigated by a class or group of students. One such topic for the intermediate grades had students design the inside of a space vehicle that would be used to transport others to colonize a planet other than earth. The students brainstormed answers to the question, "What do people need to survive?" Once a list of items was generated, categories of these items served as the basis for forming work crews. Students then chose the group in which they wished to work. The work crews searched for information associated with their areas by browsing the Internet, consulting library resources, and talking with "experts." Ultimately, a space vehicle was constructed in accordance with the specifications developed by the work groups. Students then planned and experienced their simulated day in space. More importantly, the process of topic study allows for students with varying backgrounds and skills to participate in a meaningful way (Creswell, 1997).

Topic study (storyline) is highly interactive and thoughtful. In many ways, it resembles the cognitive apprenticeship, a strategy whereby teachers or other "experts" model behaviors they hold important for students. In both instances, the teacher is a learner—more informed, perhaps, but still a learner—along with the students. As he or she coaches students toward the solution of a problem, he or she constantly looks for ways to connect with the needs of individual students.

A truly personalized approach to instruction begins and ends with the individual learner and goes well beyond the image of Mark Hopkins at one end of a log and his student James Garfield at the other. While there is nothing wrong with one-to-one instruction, even it may not be appropriate for all students some of the time and some students all of the time.

The new century requires new approaches to teaching and learning that allow students to pursue learning in teams, in groups, or alone. It expands the places for learning from within the walls of a school building to the community and even cyberspace. It establishes learning environments where students become mentors and teachers. It encourages reciprocal teaching, coaching, and tutoring with students often serving as learning preceptors for younger apprentices. It recognizes the importance of students learning how to monitor and control their own learning. It stresses self-direction and independent thought.

A persisting question facing education, therefore, is how can educators build instructional programs that focus on (1) knowing individual students as "total personalities educationally" and then creating learning environments sensitive to those differences, (2) interacting with students when they need help and as models of "experts" in action, (3) motivating students to go beyond their present level of development, and (4) identifying and encouraging creativity and self-direction? The answer may well reside in providing sufficient flexibility within the limits of federal, state, and local conditions to allow students to control and direct their learning. Certainly, new recommendations for interactive and thoughtful instructional strategies can serve as a starting point.

There is probably no greater challenge for twenty-first century educators than to raise the level of achievement for all students. The likelihood of this occurring within traditional approaches to teaching and learning is slim. What appears more reasonable, and within the reach of all schools, is the implementation of a school-redesign process focusing on the academic needs of individual students. Given the findings in cognitive science, school reform can be based on sound principles guaranteed to result in the creation of learning environments where students accept responsibility for learning, experience joy in doing so, and advance their skills to the point of being able to take the next steps in the process of lifelong learning whether it be formal education or the world of work.

CHAPTER 5

Flexible Scheduling to Promote Personalized Learning

Donald G. Hackmann

"Time is not a new issue in the education debate, but an age-old concern" (National Education Commission on Time and Learning, 1994a, p. 10).

As educators strive to create learning environments that are effective in promoting students' cognitive development, they must decide how to maximize the efficacy of the instructional day. Although any division of time is an arbitrary decision, the selection of an appropriate schedule can have significant implications for student achievement. A scheduling model can empower teachers and students to experience learning in creative, motivating ways, or it can be restrictive and repressive, forcing teachers to formulate lessons that will fit into the confines of rigid, unyielding time increments.

Scheduling can be defined as "the plan to bring together people, materials, and curriculum at a designated time and place for the purpose of instruction" (Ubben et al., 2001, p. 247). Some administrators mistakenly assume that identifying a scheduling model is the first step in the instructional design process. However, in reality, the purpose of the schedule "is to coordinate the requirements laid down by previously reached decisions regarding curriculum, instruction, grouping, and staffing" (Ubben et al., 2001, p. 247). Consequently, this decision represents the final step in this procedure: The schedule is the vehicle for delivering the curriculum, so that students can achieve mastery of content. Improved student achievement is the goal of an effective scheduling model.

This chapter provides a historical and pedagogical foundation for school scheduling, reviews scheduling approaches that were utilized through the MSP, and shares contemporary models that promote personalized learning environments. Because elementary schools traditionally provide tremendous flexibility in the self-contained classroom, in which a single teacher is responsible for delivering instruction in the core subjects and is empowered to make instructional decisions within her/his class, this chapter focuses only on middle level and secondary schools.

HISTORICAL DEVELOPMENT OF SCHEDULING MODELS: LATE 1800s TO 1960s

In the late 1800s, American secondary school schedules were characterized by great variation and instructional flexibility. Students routinely participated in learning experiences that were offered in diverse formats; each course differed in the amount of time allocated for instructional activities, and in the number of days each week in which instruction was held (Gorman, 1971). This variability, however, was problematic for college officials, who found it difficult to determine the breadth and depth of student preparation in the core disciplines. Consequently, the Committee of Ten on Secondary School Studies proposed rigid subject sequencing of college preparation courses in 1892, so that high school curricula could become standardized. This recommendation was followed in 1895, when the Committee on College Entrance Requirements suggested standardizing the number of credits required for college entry. Then, the College Entrance Examination Board adopted the Carnegie unit in 1909, which mandated 120 hours of classroom instruction, based upon class sessions of 40–60 minutes and a school year of 36–40 weeks (McNeil, 1996; Ornstein & Hunkins, 1998).

The movement toward scheduling conformity was influenced in the early 1900s by the scientific management era, which emphasized efficiency and work uniformity. As school enrollments expanded rapidly during this time, uniform scheduling models were advanced as an organizational solution to the problem of educating mass numbers of students, although educators were not particularly concerned about individual students' learning needs. Ellwood Cubberly (1916), a former superintendent of schools and Stanford University professor, noted this concern for efficiency over effectiveness: "Our schools are in a sense, factories in which the raw products (children) are to be shaped and fashioned into products to meet the various demands of life" (p. 388). The daily-period schedule was created during this era, in which the school day was divided into six, seven, or eight uniform periods, each session lasting between 40 and 60 minutes.

Daily-period schedules, with their perceived factory-model efficiency, remained the norm in the nation's middle level and secondary schools for the first half of the twentieth century. In the mid-twentieth century, however, educators began to experiment with more flexible instructional approaches.

MODULAR SCHEDULING AND THE MODEL SCHOOLS PROJECT

Championed by J. Lloyd Trump, flexible modular scheduling appeared on the secondary school scene in the late 1950s and early 1960s. With this model, the instructional day was carved into 15-, 20-, or 30-minute modules, with the total schedule containing 12, 16, or 24 daily modules (Trump & Miller, 1979). Each course could be assigned a different number of modules, depending on the types of instructional activities planned (i.e., direct instruction, demonstrations, laboratory, or small-group activities). Classes potentially could meet daily or on alternating days, with the number of assigned modules varying with each class session (Trump & Baynham, 1961). The crowning feature of this model is its tremendous instructional flexibility, although Trump and Miller (1979) cautioned that this approach also could become rigid if teachers and administrators did not take advantage of its pliable nature.

In its heyday, modular scheduling was employed in approximately 15% of American secondary schools in the late 1960s and early 1970s (Goldman, 1983). This model was perceived as effective, yet many school leaders found it quite difficult to design efficient master schedules that fully utilized the instructional flexibility inherent in the modules. Consequently, large numbers of students were not scheduled into classes at various points during the school day, which resulted in potential supervisory and disciplinary problems. Although this unscheduled time could be used for IS, if teachers were unavailable to oversee this independent work, students would not fully utilize this time. In addition, not all teachers were effective in adapting their instructional methods to the varying module lengths. Although some schools continue to use modular scheduling, this model had faded in popularity by the early 1980s, with most schools returning to daily-period approaches (Goldman, 1983).

CHARACTERISTICS OF MODEL SCHOOLS PROJECT SCHEDULES

Schools participating in the MSP in the late 1960s and early 1970s piloted numerous scheduling innovations, in an effort to provide more effective learning experiences for students. During this time, J. Lloyd Trump and his colleagues published several reports describing how the school day could be more flexibly arranged and utilized in a more productive fashion. However, Trump (1977) asserted that simply changing the schedule would not be sufficient if educators did not make basic changes in their programs and instructional methods. In describing a school for every student, Trump noted that the school environment should achieve personalization for students and staff. To ensure that each learner received individualized attention, he recommended that every student should be assigned a teacher-adviser. Any scheduling adjustments should incorporate these two characteristics of personalization and adviser-advisee relationships.

Trump and Miller (1979) noted, "The goal of the schedule is to give teachers and students as much freedom as is reasonable in the use of time, space, and numbers of persons, as well as content for instruction" (p. 397). In achieving this goal, a variety of flexible scheduling options could be employed, including year-round schooling, modular scheduling, rotating periods of different lengths or offered on different days, or team teaching arrangements. Trump and Miller cautioned, however, that even these schedules could become permanently entrenched and excessively rigid, if staff members became enamored with their new "flexible" schedules. Teachers should adjust their schedules on a regular basis, dependent upon the time necessary to successfully deliver content and to address student learning needs. Simply stated, "time varies with the purposes of teaching and learning" (Trump & Miller, 1979, p. 414).

Working with the MSP schools, Trump (1969) envisioned eight areas of study: English language arts; social sciences; mathematics; sciences; health, fitness, and recreation; fine arts; practical arts; and language arts of another country. Each week, students would be required to attend eight 30-minute large group presentations and eight 30-minute small group discussions (consisting of no more than 15 students) focused on the eight areas of knowledge. The remaining 22 hours would be devoted to IS, "scheduled by his teacher-counselor and himself in places inside the school and in the community" (Trump, 1969, pp. 128–129). Defined "simply as what pupils do when their teachers stop talking" (Trump, 1969, p. 126), IS was conceptualized as high quality activities that facilitated the individual's understanding of essential learning concepts. Pupils might be engaged in individual work, or they may be involved in cooperative learning and other SG activities.

In innovative schools, teachers were to be scheduled with groups of students for approximately 10 hours weekly. Teachers were encouraged to dramatically reduce the amount of time they were engaged in direct instruction with their entire group of students, so that teacher talk totaled to less than 20% of allocated instructional time (Trump, 1977; Trump & Georgiades, 1970). Direct instruction was to be employed in large group presentations only to give motivational talks, provide information that was unavailable elsewhere, or make oral assignments (Trump & Georgiades, 1970). Teachers also facilitated SGD of student groups of 15 or less. The remainder of the teacher's day would be spent on lesson preparation, planning for IS, conferring with colleagues, and assisting students needing special help (Trump, 1969; Trump & Georgiades, 1978).

A basic characteristic of MSP schools was the opportunity for individualized learning methods, which emphasized motivation, self-directed learning, continuous progress, and personal self-assessments (Trump & Georgiades, 1970). As Trump (1969) noted: "Even though teachers inspire better motivation and provide materials for self-directed study and appraisal, the pupils still will be limited if a flexible schedule does not release them from regularly scheduled groups for 60–70 percent of the school week" (p. 119). Such independent work was not to come at the expense of student achievement, however, as students were to be held accountable for learning. Each teacher was an adviser for approximately 35 students, developing a personal relationship with them and scheduling their IS opportunities (Trump, 1969).

It is axiomatic that restructuring the traditional teacher workweek to include a maximum of only 10 hours for instruction would necessitate the employment of additional personnel to work closely with students during their independent activities. To satisfy this requirement without increasing personnel costs, Trump (1969, 1977) recommended reducing the number of teachers and creating a differentiated instructional support staff consisting of full-time teachers and part-time instructional assistants, clerks, and general aides. Each full-time teacher would be provided with the weekly equivalent of 20 hours of instructional assistant services, 10 hours of clerical assistance, and 5 hours of general aide services. In addition, a cadre of volunteers who were community members also could assist in the school. A differentiated guidance arrangement also could be initiated, consisting of teacher-advisers, professional counselors, and special consultants (Trump, 1977).

Individualized education was the instructional goal of the MSP. Recognizing that individualization is a lofty aspiration, Trump and Georgiades (1978) suggested that schools consider using a Pontoon Transition design as a two-year transition toward this goal. Pontoon plans utilized flexible blocks of time for LG presentations, SGD, and individual study. Adamant in their support for personalized learning environments, they avowed, "There is no room in a good instructional program for the traditional class of from 25 to 35 students" (Trump & Georgiades, 1978, p. 121).

CALLS FOR SCHEDULING REFORM AND THE EMERGENCE OF CONSTRUCTIVIST THEORY

The educational accountability movement that began with the publication of *A Nation at Risk* (National Commission on Excellence in Education, 1984) 20 years ago released an onslaught of calls for school reforms that have continued through the present time. One concern that has emerged in the national debate has been the seemingly rigid way in which secondary schools have approached the instructional day. The National Education Commission on Time and Learning (NECTL, 1994a) was critical of uniform daily-period scheduling models that were present in the majority of the nation's secondary schools, noting, "The degree to which today's American school is controlled by the dynamics of clock and calendar is surprising" (p. 7). The NASSP (1996) was more scathing in its criticism: "Right now, in most high schools, the schedule is frozen, glacier-like, into 50-minute segments that dictate the amount of instructional time devoted to each course, regardless of what would be most appropriate on a particular day" (p. 47).

Reform advocates have suggested that schools should be restructured around learning, rather than the seat-time mandates of the Carnegie unit (NASSP, 1996; NECTL, 1994a). Echoing Trump's (1977) recommendations for a more personalized curriculum, English (1993) argued for a learner-centered schedule with few school boundaries, permitting student learning opportunities to be expanded into the community. So that teachers could work more closely with students, NECTL (1994a) proposed the use of block-of-time schedules, other flexible scheduling arrangements, and team teaching.

Other national reports have provided additional recommendations to repair design flaws that existed in many schools, including providing more time-on-task, reducing rote learning methods, reducing seatwork, and increasing teaching methods that actively engage students in learning (NECTL, 1994b). Noting that elementary, middle, and secondary schools each addressed varying development needs of students, the NECTL (1994c) recommended different organizational and instructional approaches for each level. However, administrators were reminded to ensure that sufficient time for professional development was a significant consideration for teachers at all school levels.

CONSTRUCTIVIST THEORY EMERGES

Heeding the calls for school reform, educators have began to shift away from behaviorist approaches to instruction, which regard teaching as being highly diagnostic and prescriptive activity. Under behaviorist models, curriculum content is broken down into small but manageable increments, with student practice immediately following each teaching episode. Characterized by direct instruction methods, behaviorism tends to place primary emphasis on the teachers' role in the instructional process.

Building upon the early work of Jean Piaget and Lev Vygotsky, an extensive body of research on cognitive processing has been developed since the late 1980s, which emphasizes the student's role as an active and engaged participant in the process of learning (Brooks & Brooks, 1993). Advocates for this approach, which is known as constructivist theory, promote learning as a social activity, in which the learner actively creates, or "constructs," meaning through the process of experiencing and discussing curriculum concepts. Instead of being the primary distribution point for knowledge through the traditional lecture method, teachers using constructivist approaches become facilitators of learning. Students are encouraged to apply concepts through real-word, context-bound experiences, including such activities as problem-based learning, interdisciplinary instruction, and cooperative learning. Because depth of understanding is more important than surface treatment of subject matter, constructivists recommend that the curriculum be narrowed to permit teachers to focus on mastery of essential knowledge and skills. Metacognition is a consistent theme throughout these experiences (Glatthorn, 1995).

Although they have not directly cited constructivist theory in their documents, many professional organizations reference principles of constructivism in their recommendations regarding the teaching-learning process. For example, in suggesting numerous reforms for twenty-first century high schools, NASSP (1996) promoted the "teacher as coach" metaphor, so that students would be engaged in hands-on learning activities. Two principles of the CES (2002a), "student as worker, teacher as coach" and "less is more," also refer to constructivist beliefs. In creating learner-centered classrooms, however, teachers should be aware of the dangers of excessive reliance on either behaviorist or constructivist practices. Direct instruction certainly is pedagogically sound in certain instructional situations, and hands-on activities are not always easily developed in every subject (Airasian & Walsh, 1997). Teachers should strive to maintain an appropriate balance, so that teacher instruction and student-centered activities complement one another and promote student content mastery.

As educators strive to create learner-centered environments, they quickly recognize that daily-period scheduling models restrict teachers' creativity and flexibility to design engaging lessons. Larger blocks of time are necessary to facilitate the use of constructivist activities (Elmore, 1995; Windschitl, 1999), and to develop cross-disciplinary instructional approaches. The NASSP (1996) *Breaking Ranks* report presented this argument for flexible scheduling to meet individual students' needs:

> High schools should create more flexible schedules—compatible with learning objectives—to make it easier for each student to meet the requirements of the curriculum. What we have in mind is the kind of flexibility that serves learning by organizing instruction in ways more friendly to teaching and learning. (p. 47)

CURRENT TRENDS IN SECONDARY SCHEDULING

Acknowledging that daily-period models can cause excessive fragmentation of the instructional day, some high school educators began to question the effectiveness of this scheduling approach in the 1980s. Because teachers often are assigned to teach in excess of 180 students in the daily-period structure, creating personalized learning environments can be exceedingly difficult to attain at the secondary level. Daily-period models also can contribute to teachers' overreliance on lecturing, restrict teachers' ability to collaborate in delivering interdisciplinary instruction, and discourage in-depth study of curriculum content.

Experimentation with various forms of block-of-time scheduling models, which typically utilize 80–95 minute timeframes for each course, initially began in the late 1980s and rapidly gained momentum throughout the 1990s. In 1999 Rettig and Canady estimated that approximately 30% of high schools employ some form of block-of-time scheduling, and this percentage is likely somewhat higher today. The two most commonly used forms of block schedules are the 4×4 semester plan and the eight-block alternating-day model, both of which will be described later in this chapter.

The current block-scheduling formats do not provide the degree of flexibility achieved through modular scheduling or the individualization advocated by Trump, but they are more responsive to the formation of constructivist lessons and personalized learning environments than daily-period models. Schools using block schedules have reported numerous positive results, including decreased student disciplinary referral and suspensions, improved teacher-student relationships, improved attendance, a more relaxed learning environment, and more active student involvement in instruction (Buckman, King, & Ryan, 1995; Hackmann, 1995; Wilson, 1995). Of course, teachers cannot simply consider a block session as merely a double-period class and continue to employ behaviorist teaching methods. If teachers do not fully embrace constructivist strategies, students will find it extremely difficult to maintain their attention levels when forced to sit through a 90-minute lecture. Consequently, extensive professional development is needed to provide teachers with the skills to utilize a variety of effective instructional strategies within the larger timeframes (Hackmann & Schmitt, 1997).

This section shares common high school models that utilize blocks, either exclusively or in combination with traditional daily-period arrangements. To reinforce the importance of teacher advisors in forming close relationships with students and personalization, each example will include time for advisory/homeroom activities. To remain consistent with Trump's (1969) recommendation of eight areas of study, all scheduling examples throughout this section will be based on each student enrolling in eight courses in an academic year. The current literature base is filled with examples of secondary- and middle-level scheduling configurations, and the reader is encouraged to consult this extensive database for more comprehensive explanation of the format, strengths, and limitations of each of these approaches.

4×4 Semester Plan

With the 4×4 semester model, classes are scheduled in instructional blocks, typically lasting approximately 90 minutes each, which meet for only one-half of the school year (Canady & Rettig, 1995). Each student enrolls in four daily courses the first semester and an additional four the second semester, totaling eight courses for the entire academic year. Carroll's (1989) Copernican plan is similar to the 4×4 approach, but it utilizes a trimester configuration that permits students to complete nine courses in a school year.

One of the principles of the CES (2002b) is the goal of personalization, in that teachers would be responsible for no more than 80 students. The 4×4 model can achieve this goal, because teachers would teach only three courses each semester, in contrast with six or seven classes under the traditional daily-period model. Consequently, students and teachers have the opportunity to form closer bonds, and teachers are more likely to gain a more complete understanding of each individual student's learning needs.

Many secondary educators favor the 4×4 model, because it permits students to focus on a limited number of subjects each semester, promoting intensive and in-depth study in these disciplines. However, others oppose this model, because they argue that massed practice over a few months is less effective than learning opportunities spaced throughout the academic year. For critics, a significant concern is the potential retention loss due to several months that may pass between sequenced subjects; for example, if a student completes the initial algebra course in the first semester of her/his freshman year, but is not enrolled in the second mathematics course until the second semester of the sophomore year. Another concern is the "one size fits all" approach used by some secondary school faculties, in which all courses are forced into the semester format, even though this approach may not be the preferred instructional alternative. For example, teachers of courses such as instrumental music, chorus, journalism, to name a few, may wish to hold their classes throughout the entire academic year. In the "pure" 4×4 format, these classes either must be held only one semester, or the student must enroll in two blocks throughout the year; in the latter instance, one-fourth of the student's course load would be dedicated to only one class.

To be more responsive to the unique characteristics of some academic disciplines, some schools choose to modify the 4×4 format. One alternative is the 3×3 plan, in which students enroll in three blocked courses each semester and one course (typically called a "skinny") that meets in a 45-minute format throughout the year, for a total of seven courses. Schools also could utilize a 3×3 approach that includes two year-long "skinnies," so that students may complete eight courses. Each of these alternatives, however, forces every student to complete the same number of blocked and daily-period courses, which still retains the rigidity and uniformity that critics detested in the traditional daily-period models.

Table 5.1 provides an example of a "pure" 4×4 semester model that includes 90-minute class sessions, a daily 25-minute teacher advisory period, and a whole-school lunch period. Obviously, this schedule merely is provided for illustration purposes. School officials may choose to schedule the advisory period at another time in the day and also may need to schedule numerous lunch periods to accommodate their student body in their cafeteria facilities. Also, they may choose to "break up" any block, permitting the scheduling of year-long courses as needed.

Alternating-Day Block Schedule

The alternating-day schedule affords instruction in one-half of the school's schedule of classes on a two-day cycle. Currently, the most commonly used alternating-day model enrolls students in eight classes throughout the entire academic year, with blocks 1–4 and 5–8 rotating every other day. This approach sometimes is called the A/B schedule, because the alternating days are often labeled "A" and "B" days, to help teachers and students recall which courses are being held on a given day. The model technically uses a two-day cycle, but some individuals prefer to conceptualize it over the duration of two weeks: Blocks 1–4 would be held on Monday-Wednesday-Friday of week one, and Tuesday-Thursday of week two; blocks 5–8, of course, would occur on the opposing days.

When compared to the 4×4 semester plan, the alternating-day model has benefits and limitations. This model resolves the "retention loss" limitation of the 4×4 plan, because students will be enrolled in every class for an entire academic year. It permits students to focus on only

Table 5.1. 4×4 Semester Schedule: Secondary School

Time	Monday	Tuesday	Wednesday	Thursday	Friday
8:00 – 9:30	1	1	1	1	1
9:35 – 11:05	2	2	2	2	2
11:10 – 11:35	Advisory	Advisory	Advisory	Advisory	Advisory
11:40 – 12:10	Lunch	Lunch	Lunch	Lunch	Lunch
12:15 – 1:45	3	3	3	3	3
1:50 – 3:10	4	4	4	4	4

four subjects each day, and they have the additional benefit of having two evenings to complete homework assignments. However, students now must focus on eight subjects throughout the year, as opposed to in-depth study in only four subjects in the 4×4 model. In addition, the goal of personalization is not fully addressed in this model. Even though teachers instruct only half of their students each day, they still are responsible for the same large number of students that they would teach in a traditional daily-period schedule.

Because of the difficulties in recalling which days of the week a given class will be held, the alternating-day schedule can be modified so that all classes meet in a daily-period format the same day each week. For example, some faculties may decide to hold all eight classes on Mondays to provide students with an overview of the upcoming week's activities, or they may select Friday as the daily-class day, to prepare students for homework assignments for the weekend. Some districts schedule one morning or afternoon every week for teacher professional development, resulting in a "Wednesday late start" or "Tuesday early dismissal" for students, and the daily-period format could be used on this professional development day.

Table 5.2 shares an eight-block alternating-day model that includes a 20-minute morning advisory period, 90-minute blocks with all classes meeting on Monday. Other variations include the six-block model (three classes on alternating days) and the 10-block model (five classes on

Table 5.2. Alternating-Day Block Schedule: Secondary School (Daily-Period Option on Mondays)

Time	Monday	Tuesday	Wednesday	Thursday	Friday
8:00 – 8:20	Advisory	Advisory	Advisory	Advisory	Advisory
8:25 – 9:10	1	1	2	1	2
9:15 – 10:00	2				
10:05 – 10:50	3	3	4	3	4
10:55 – 11:40	4				
11:40 – 12:05	Lunch	Lunch	Lunch	Lunch	Lunch
12:10 – 12:55	5	5	6	5	6
1:00 – 1:45	6				
1:50 – 2:35	7	7	8	7	8
2:40 – 3:25	8				

alternating days). A seven-block approach occasionally is implemented, with alternating blocks 1–3 and 4–6, and the seventh class (the "skinny") that meets daily. In this instance, if the blocked classes meet for 90 minutes, the seventh class typically is 45 minutes in duration.

Combination/Hybrid Models

Some schools may adopt scheduling models that incorporate multiple features of both the daily-period and block-of-time approaches. A combination alternating-day/daily-period model could include daily periods three days each week and blocks the remaining two days. For example, all eight periods would meet on Mondays, Tuesdays, and Fridays, blocks 1–4 would be on Wednesdays, and blocks 5–8 on Thursdays. Other schools reserve the mornings for blocked classes (blocks 1–4 on either alternating days or a semester plan) and afternoons for daily periods (periods 5–8). Another alternative, which would be much more responsive to student and teacher needs, is to simultaneously operate a 4×4 semester plan and eight-period daily schedule.

Hybrid models sometimes are implemented to help teachers and students transition slowly from the daily-period models to a 4×4 or alternating-day block, not unlike the Pontoon Transition plan of Trump and Georgiades (1978), and the ultimate goal may be to fully implement a block schedule within a few years. Often, combination models attempt to provide the best of both worlds—daily periods and blocks—while providing instructional variety from one day to the next. If they are merely adopted as a compromise to partially satisfy two competing faculty camps—those preferring blocks and those desiring to maintain the daily-period approach—teachers may not utilize the instructional time to the fullest. However, if they are developed for sound pedagogical reasons, and if they can retain their characteristics of instructional flexibility, they can be very effective in providing a learner-centered environment.

Flexible Schedules with Interdisciplinary Blocks

Some secondary schools have been experimenting with interdisciplinary instruction through the use of the teaming concept that for many years has been recognized as a signature practice in middle-level schools (George & Alexander, 1993). As early as 1970, Trump and Georgiades (1970) were advocating for an interdisciplinary approach to learning, which they termed the pontoon concept, "identified as inter-relating two or more subjects under the leadership of teachers from different disciplines in a block of time in which each would ordinarily operate independently" (p. 120). Over 25 years later, the NASSP (1996) also endorsed this concept, recommending that high school teachers work in collaborative teams to break away from the subject-dominated approach to curriculum.

Teams typically may be used at the freshman—and occasionally the sophomore—level, with large blocks of time provided for some combination of English language arts, social studies, mathematics, and science. For example, a team composed of instructors from the four core areas may be assigned four clock hours daily for instruction in these disciplines. Teaching teams are empowered to divide these assigned blocks into any instructional arrangement that is necessary for a given day's instructional purposes (Hackmann & Waters, 1998). The remainder of the student's coursework may be scheduled in either a block or daily-period configuration. Interdisciplinary teaming has its roots in the middle school movement, and this approach will be more fully described in the next section. Because secondary schools typically do not require the same core subjects of all students in 11th and 12th grades, the ability to form interdisciplinary teams at these grade levels is compromised. Consequently, although it is not impossible, it would be uncommon to observe teaming arrangements in place at the upper secondary grade levels.

CURRENT TRENDS IN MIDDLE-LEVEL SCHEDULING

At the foundation of the middle school movement is the belief that responding to the needs of the emerging adolescent is of the utmost importance. As children reach puberty and enter into early adolescence, they encounter a host of rapid developmental changes: physical, cognitive, emotional, and social. Of course, these changes do not occur in a uniform fashion, either within an individual child or across a group of children. Therefore, middle-level schools are characterized by tremendous variation among students, and teachers must be adept at altering the instructional program to address a wide range of interests and abilities (Williamson, 1998).

Although the literature supports a variety of practices that are responsive to the needs of the emerging adolescent, five programmatic practices are consistently noted as essential in the design of effective middle-level schools: adviser/advisee programs, interdisciplinary teaming, the existence of an extensive array of exploratory course options for students, a variety of co-curricular offerings, and a sound intramural activities program (Valentine, Clark, Hackmann, & Petzko, 2002). Advisory programs provide an "opportunity for the personalized guidance and active monitoring young adolescents need" (Jackson & Davis, 2000, p. 143). Sadly, a recent national study of over 1,400 middle-level school principals, conducted by the NASSP, determined that only 57% of respondents provide a regularly scheduled adviser-advisee program (Valentine et al., 2002). Clearly, middle-level schools can be more effective in creating a personalized environment that permits the formation of close teacher-student bonds.

An ineffective scheduling arrangement can create insurmountable barriers to the formation of a personalized learning environment. Therefore, the following factors are offered to provide guidance to middle-level teachers and administrators as they consider the appropriate scheduling model:

1. The schedule should support interdisciplinary team organization.
2. The schedule should support an appropriate curriculum.
3. The schedule should support quality instruction in the disciplines through the expanded and flexible uses of time.
4. The schedule should promote student development and supportive relationships.
5. The schedule should promote quality teacher collaboration.
6. The school should promote teacher empowerment. (Hackmann & Valentine, 1998, pp. 3–5)

Although a scheduling approach that facilitates interdisciplinary instruction is perceived to be the epitome of the middle school schedule, only 42% of respondents to the NASSP middle-level study reported utilizing this approach (Valentine et al., 2002). Interestingly, this study also determined that 79% of these schools reported having interdisciplinary teaming in place. Consequently, many middle school teachers are challenged to find creative ways to achieve curriculum integration while working within the confines of a subject-based scheduling model.

When designing effective middle-level schedules, administrators should arm teachers with the authority to collaboratively make instructional decisions related to how their blocks of time will be arranged each day. Teachers, however, must be willing to rearrange the day to facilitate instructional strategies that address their students' learning needs. Otherwise, as Trump and Miller (1979) had cautioned against, these flexible models can suffer the same fate as the rigid daily-period scheduling models of years past, remaining the same from one day to the next.

The development of high-quality teams mandates that common planning time must be provided, so that teachers have sufficient time to plan integrated lessons, decide how to schedule the instructional day, conference with students and parents, discuss individual student needs, and solve any problems that may arise (Valentine et al., 2002). Flowers, Mertens, and Mulhall (2000) note that teams with high amounts of common planning time are more likely to integrate the curriculum and to view their group activities in a positive fashion. To ensure that teachers have sufficient preparation time to meet both their collaborative and personal professional needs, both common and individual planning time must be scheduled. Unfortunately, only 59% of principals responding to the NASSP study reported that both common and individual planning times were provided to teachers (Valentine et al., 2002). Clearly, there is room for improvement.

Middle-level educators will note that secondary school teachers and administrators now are being encouraged to adopt practices that are at the core of the middle school philosophy, such as the interdisciplinary teaming, adviser/advisee, and personalization that are noted in the National Middle School Association's (1995) document, *This We Believe.* Although it is true that numerous middle-level practices can be equally successful at the secondary level, not all secondary practices are appropriate for the middle level. For example, the perceived success of high school faculties in implementing block scheduling has led many of the nation's middle-level faculties to adopt models that parrot their secondary counterparts, but some formats (in particular, the 4×4 semester plan) do not permit flexible uses of time for interdisciplinary teaming. Middle-level teachers and administrators should be cautious when considering secondary models, to ensure that they remain true to the middle school philosophy (Hackmann, 2002). Because the importance of interdisciplinary teaming and adviser-advisee programs, this section will describe only scheduling models that incorporate these two elements.

Flexible Interdisciplinary Schedule with Daily Periods

The flexible interdisciplinary schedule, often called the flexible block schedule or interdisciplinary block schedule, is considered to be the basic organizational framework of the exemplary middle-level school (George & Alexander, 1993). One criticism of scheduling models in general is that each subject often is allocated an identical amount of time for instruction, when this approach is not necessary or even desirable. For example, in this era of accountability to document student mastery of state content standards, teachers and administrators may wish to provide more instructional time for core classes (English language arts, social studies, math, and science) than for other subjects.

With the flexible interdisciplinary schedule, blocks of time are set aside for teaching teams, and teachers who take full advantage of this opportunity may choose to dedicate more time to selected subjects. Teams may choose to provide instruction in the core classes daily, on an alternating-day basis, or an as-needed basis. Teams may consist of as few as two teachers or as many as six or more teachers, although data from the NASSP middle-level study found four-person teams to be the most commonly utilized (Valentine et al., 2002). The majority of schools include five courses (English language arts, social studies, mathematics, science, reading) or four courses (English language arts, social studies, mathematics, reading) in the teaming block, but other teaming arrangements, of course can be developed. Team subjects are included in the core instructional block, and the remaining subjects are scheduled using a daily-period approach.

Table 5.3 shares an example of a flexible interdisciplinary block schedule that includes the four core subjects within the teaming block and four additional subjects in a daily-period arrangement, permitting the student to complete eight courses throughout the academic year. For illustration purposes only, this example shows a sample student's schedule that includes an exploratory wheel, music or other elective, physical education, and reading. Thirty-eight percent of respondents to the NASSP middle-level study reported using a daily interdisciplinary model (Valentine et al., 2002).

Alternating-Day Flexible Interdisciplinary Schedule

For teachers who subscribe to constructivist theory, there is one criticism with the flexible interdisciplinary schedule that utilizes daily periods. While this model is very responsive to providing creative uses of time for teachers of core classes within the block, teachers of non-core (or "encore") subjects still must adhere to the uniform 45-minute daily-period timeframes. Arguably, teachers of courses such as family/consumer science, technology education, physical education, and art, to name just a few disciplines, would find timeframes of approximately 90 minutes to be more beneficial, so that students could be engaged in projects, laboratory activities, demonstrations, and other hands-on learning activities.

Table 5.3.   Flexible Interdisciplinary Schedule with Daily Periods: Middle-Level Schedule

Time	Monday	Tuesday	Wednesday	Thursday	Friday
8:00 – 8:20	Advisory	Advisory	Advisory	Advisory	Advisory
8:25 – 9:10					
9:15 – 10:00	Core	Core	Core	Core	Core
10:05 – 10:50	Block	Block	Block	Block	Block
10:55 – 11:40					
11:40 – 12:05	Lunch	Lunch	Lunch	Lunch	Lunch
12:10 – 12:55	Exploratory	Exploratory	Exploratory	Exploratory	Exploratory
1:00 – 1:45	Music/ Elective	Music/ Elective	Music/ Elective	Music/ Elective	Music/ Elective
1:50 – 2:35	Physical Education	Physical Education	Physical Education	Physical Education	Physical Education
2:40 – 3:25	Reading	Reading	Reading	Reading	Reading

NOTE: Core Block includes English language arts, social studies, mathematics, and science.

Key:

☐ = Interdisciplinary Block

Taking a cue from the apparent success of the eight-block alternating-day scheduling models and their variations that are being employed at the secondary level, many middle-level schools have now adopted the high school model that is illustrated in Table 5.2. Although this approach permits some cross-disciplinary connections, it does not provide the tremendous flexibility that is desired in truly interdisciplinary models. What is needed, therefore, is a model that provides the capacity for interdisciplinary instruction, retains block options for all subjects, and grants instructional flexibility for the teaming subjects.

The alternating-day flexible interdisciplinary schedule, which is displayed in Table 5.4, satisfies all of the aforementioned criteria. For illustration purposes, the interdisciplinary teaming block encompasses the four core subjects (English language arts, social studies, mathematics, and science) and provides four additional blocked subjects that meet on an alternating-day basis. This student example includes the same "encore"

Table 5.4.   Alternating-Day Flexible Interdisciplinary Schedule: Middle-Level Schedule (Daily Period Option on Mondays)

Time	Monday	Tuesday	Wednesday	Thursday	Friday
8:00 – 8:20	Advisory	Advisory	Advisory	Advisory	Advisory
8:25 – 9:10	Math	Math	Social Studies	Math	Social Studies
9:15 – 10:00	Social Studies				
10:05 – 10:50	Science	Science	Language Arts	Science	Language Arts
10:55 – 11:40	Language Arts				
11:40 – 12:05	Lunch	Lunch	Lunch	Lunch	Lunch
12:10 – 12:55	Reading	Reading	Exploratory	Reading	Exploratory
1:00 – 1:45	Exploratory				
1:50 – 2:35	Band	Band	Physical Education	Band	Physical Education
2:40 – 3:25	Physical Education				

Key:

[ ] = Interdisciplinary Block

courses as shown in the preceding table. Similar to the secondary school alternating-day model illustrated in Table 5.2, this example also includes the daily-period option, in which all eight classes meet on Mondays.

This alternating-day option provides the same degree of flexibility for interdisciplinary team teachers as the Table 5.3 option: Teams may choose to have all four classes meet daily, on an alternating-day basis, or any other configuration that meets the instructional needs of the team. However, this model provides the additional benefit of blocking the "encore" classes, so that all teachers in the school are empowered to teach in larger timeframes.

CONCLUSION

Although they may not yet have fully achieved Trump's vision of individualized education and personalization, the middle-level and secondary scheduling models currently being employed in many schools come much closer to these goals than the daily-period models of the 1960s and 1970s. Regardless of the scheduling approach that is agreed upon by a school's faculty, it should ensure that teachers are empowered to adjust their instructional units in ways that ensure the maximum use of time. In addition, these scheduling approaches should permit teachers to utilize constructivist instructional strategies, so that students have continual opportunities to be actively engaged in the process of learning: thinking, problem solving, experiencing, and talking about their work. These models also should ensure opportunities for student engagement within the community, for individual study, and for one-on-one interactions between teacher and student.

In many ways, today's scheduling models are characterized by greater variety than was the case throughout the majority of the twentieth century. Although variety can be perceived as a positive feature, however, it is not the definitive goal of an effective model. The ultimate aim of the schedule is to promote improved student achievement—to create a personalized environment in which every child learns well. Teachers and administrators should keep this purpose in mind as they decide the most effective way to structure the school day.

CHAPTER 6

Personalizing the Curriculum

Fenwick W. English and James W. Keefe

Preparing for state-mandated testing is the operative principal in much of contemporary curriculum design. Even the time-honored if dubious tradition of "content coverage" has been overwhelmed by the rush to "teach to the test." It has not always been so. One has only to look at the curriculum paradigm proposed by the MSP to understand that the ideology of the present would be foreign to many innovators of the past. The purpose of this chapter is to explain the personalized framework by which curriculum was addressed in the NASSP MSP, and to show how the LECI and others have extended this framework to include thematic and exhibition-based curriculum, authentic pedagogy, apprenticeships, and so forth. Further, the chapter will examine the current state of curriculum planning and assessment and compare it with personalized approaches.

The challenges facing educators in personalizing curriculum and instruction have never been greater. Prior to current state-imposed accountability schemes, the only obstacles to a more personalized education were tradition and self-imposed mental boxes about what should be required for schooling. Critical tensions have always existed between the values of personalized education and those of government centered on uniformity and efficiency in delivering a state-designed set of educational outcomes. Personalization requires choice on the part of the student, but not a completely open set of choices. Choices are set within a range of options. The more important perspective is that the essential humanness of each person is centered rather than subordinated to other interests. The development of the human remains the central purpose of a personalized education.

The two major perspectives dominating curriculum discourse are presented as opposite poles in Figure 6.1. What is portrayed here are not only practices but the belief systems in which they are embedded. The perspective with a longer history in Western tradition emanates from the humanities, the arts and sciences. That perspective resonates to the idea of the ancient sophists that "man is the measure of all things." Current state educational accountability schemes make "the measurement of man all things."

The column on the left in Figure 6.1 represents the values and actions of nearly all the state-imposed accountability schemes in the United States today. The right column represents the antipode or opposite

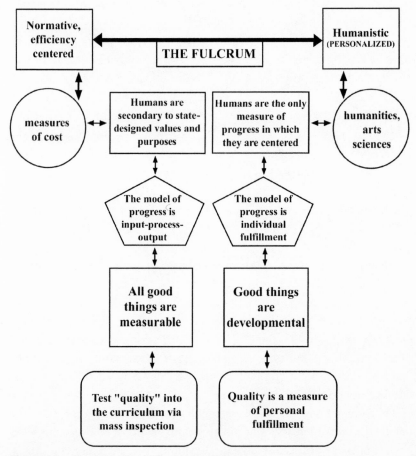

Figure 6.1.   *The Antipodes of Curriculum Discourse*

model of humanistic, personalized progress and fulfillment. The creation of state standards, state curricular frameworks, benchmarks, and learning "indicators" are the things "to be acquired" by all students. In the new federal law, the No Child Left Behind Act, "no child" means no exceptions. The inclusiveness of state systems serves notice to educators that while there may be differences among students, they can't be significant enough to allow for any exceptions. This underlying notion represents the subordination of human interests to the interests of system values and priorities. "Differences" are marginalized or controlled in order to enable schools to pump out a "no defects" model of education. Differences are not to be celebrated, but eliminated. They are not cherished earmarks of humanity; they represent "challenges" to be overcome. Metaphors of manufacturing overwhelmingly dominate in state systems of educational accountability. And the kind of measurement widespread in such systems is ruthlessly suppressive of cultural, linguistic, and creative differences among peoples and subcultures. Differences are not seen as critical or important enough to be recognized or exempted (Dantley, 1990).

Unfortunately, nearly all state accountability schemes are still aimed at minimal competency testing. And student choice has been eliminated as anything remotely necessary or even desirable. Those of us who have been in some of the nation's schools preparing for the state's minimal competency testing have been witness to the drill and boredom which are the accoutrements of an approach to schooling in which student interest is not a factor. Instead, the burden of keeping students interested in testing (and the learning that will be tested) has fallen on teachers and administrators. It is their responsibility to make things interesting. Many have resorted to such devices as student pep rallies, contests between classes, and other bizarre challenges. One school principal sat on the roof of the school for a while because that is what her students wanted if they became "test busters."

The underlying premise of an efficiency-focused, rational-technical model of education fits nicely into an economic model that examines only inputs-processes-outputs. The fact that "outcomes" cannot be divorced from their conceptualization and use is rarely considered. In her review of the huge collapses of Enron, Arthur Andersen, and WorldCom, former Harvard Business School professor Barbara Ley Toffler

(2003) noted that "Enron, Andersen, and WorldCom all had principles and ethics codes that ostensibly guided their behavior. Each had a Web site prominently displaying their carefully crafted visions. Yet they all ultimately failed" (p. 240). Companies fail because they lose a sense of values about what is important. They forget about trust and integrity. When the only thing that matters is whether the stock goes up or not, and everything is sacrificed to that end (O'Boyle, 1998), we have the enshrinement of the input-process-output model. In education, we see that model operating when the attainment of outputs (test scores) becomes subordinate to virtually everything elsess—even when that may mean the loss of significant chunks of curriculum, the reification of teacher-directed models of instruction centered on the acquisition of facts, and the abandonment of any approach that centers the individual human as the goal of education.

THE VALUES OF PERSONALIZED EDUCATION

Personalized education has a long history in the West. Its roots extend to the humanism of pre-Socratic Greek philosophers such as Heraclitus, and continue with the writings of Plato and the establishment of his Academy. The Greeks were primarily interested in questions regarding reality and the meaning of human actions. Education was an individual pursuit directed at confronting both the questions and the possible answers to lifelong moral and civic dilemmas. Education was conceptualized as a journey, a pursuit of things of value. The Greeks envisioned education as what we today could call a *transformative experience*, one that could not be easily programmed. At the center of the Greek experience stood the individual human being, something sacred and beautiful. The student occupied the center in this model. Education was something that, while prescriptive, did not subordinate the student to the needs of the state (except perhaps for Sparta, where children were brought up to perpetuate a military monarchy).

Today's state accountability plans are very much Spartan in outlook. The student is the instrument of the state, to be "done with and done to" so that he/she has the "required proficiencies" according to prespecified milestones. Mass inspection by standardized testing dominates current educational decision making. Testing dates are fixed arbitrarily and administratively; that is, the selection of the dates has little to do with student learning curves or growth patterns. The testing system is designed so that the state educational bureaucracy can make decisions about "school quality." Testing must support the bureaucratic machinery and students, learning, and teaching are subordinated to the bureaucracy. For example, when students have shown that they have mastered the curricular material on a benchmark test, but it is still quite some time until the state's designated testing time, schools are forced to make provision for reviews to refresh students at some immediate point prior to the state assessment.

THE MODEL SCHOOLS PROJECT CURRICULUM

The NASSP MSP is an early example of personalized education. With eight areas of knowledge and three levels of student mastery, student choice was an integral part of the MSP curriculum paradigm. Looking back even earlier, the Eight-Year Study of the 1930s (Aiken, 1942) was a seminal influence on the thinking and professional practice of J. Lloyd Trump, director of the NASSP MSP. The Eight-Year Study was commissioned by the Progressive Education Association in 1930 to explore means of better coordination between high school and college work and to enable high schools "to attempt fundamental reconstruction." Thirty high schools participated. Members of the Commission agreed that high schools needed "experimental study and comprehensive re-examination" in 18 areas, including curriculum. The Commission, among other determinations, observed that "The conventional high school curriculum was far removed from the real concerns of youth," and that "The traditional subjects of the curriculum had lost much of their vitality and significance." Two school principals in this Eight-Year Study later served on Trump's Commission on the Experimental Study of the Utilization of the Staff in the Secondary School, from 1956 to 1960. And many of the same areas identified for exploration in the earlier study would emerge in the "Trump Plan" of the 1960s and the MSP of the 1970s.

The MSP proposed a threefold rationale for curriculum content (NASSP, 1969); the MSP curriculum was to include:

1. What was essential for everyone to know in all subject areas and required of all (the "basic" program);
2. Hobbies (special interests) that result when the student is motivated to learn more of the subject than is essential, in greater depth and/or to be creative (electives and special studies—the "desirable" program); and
3. Careers that are open to students who go beyond the essential and hobby levels (college and vocational preparation—the "enriching" or "quest" program).

In addition, all MSP students were required to have *continual contact* with eight areas of learning (nine in religious schools):

- English
- Fine Arts
- Foreign Culture (languages)
- Health, Fitness, Recreation (physical education)
- Mathematics
- Practical Arts
- Science
- Social Studies

Trump (1969, p. 127) argued that the curriculum needed to

attack positively some weaknesses in today's organization of content: (a) the need for more continuous contact for all pupils with the essential materials in all areas of human knowledge; (b) the need for more time and opportunities for each pupil to develop his special talents and interests; (c) the need for materials which satisfy both (a) and (b), which permit each pupil to progress continuously at a rate that is best for him, and which also measure his achievement satisfactorily; (d) the need to select content more nearly related to the *real* world of pupils and less to the specialized, as it seems to pupils, *make-believe* world of the teacher; and (e) the need to utilize community resources in the learning process.

Trump went on to point out that the curriculum of the day tended to emphasize what professors and subject-matter specialists felt was most important, whether a given student or group of students needed the content or not. Since not every student would become a professional mathematician, scientist, or writer, not everyone needed more advanced work in those fields. The "basic" curriculum, then, would embrace what was *essential for all students*. The more desirable and enriching levels of curriculum would be made available to those with special interests and talents. And both the basic and in-depth content "should be organized for self-pacing, continuous progressing, and self-evaluating by pupils with a minimum of teacher supervision."

MSP students were asked to devote the majority of their time in elementary and middle-level schooling to their basic or essential education, with some in-depth study as special talents and interests dictated. High school students would spend much of their time on desirable and enriching tasks. This process of continuing contact with the essential learning and gradual immersion in in-depth studies would "enable the student to see the eight areas of knowledge as part of the daily world in which he lives rather than as isolated subjects which he will study in a few required classes and then dismiss from his mind forever" (Trump, 1969, p. 128).

Specific recommendations of the MSP called for one 30-minute presentation and one 30-minute SGD each week in each of the eight areas of knowledge, and an otherwise truly flexible schedule with 20 hours per week of IS, scheduled by a teacher-adviser, both in the school and in the community. IS was viewed as "what students do when teachers stop talking." Each student's schedule was individualized to reflect personal talents and interests, and to motivate the student toward achieving his or her present and future goals. At the onset of the project, the large and small groups were envisioned as primarily "motivational," but evolved in many schools to be content-oriented, with an instructional purpose, and for the small groups, with a seminar or cooperative small-group format.

The curriculum was individualized in units and designed for continuous progress. Individual materials for each unit were made available to students in the form of learning packets referenced with books, pamphlets, teacher-prepared materials, models, audio-visual media, community and work experiences, as well as unit self-, pre- and post-tests. Students worked through a defined sequence of learning units/packets in each required or in-depth area of learning, taking curriculum-referenced or performance tests, when ready, to show that they had mastered the required knowledge or skill. Students could challenge units immediately if they were already competent to take the qualifying test(s), or seek teacher or peer tutoring for units in which they needed special assistance. They could take as much time, within reason, as they needed to complete the basic and optional units of their programs of study. Slower students merely needed and took more time.

The MSP vision of schooling was radically different from what occurs in traditional schools. The aim was to assist learners to find their niches and to remember their schooling as so pleasant that, years later, they might discover a hobby or special interest in some field that did not occupy their adult life. Trump (1977) put it this way:

> The goal is for as many persons as possible to continue to want to learn as long as they live. . . . Repeatedly we emphasize that a school for everyone provides alternatives. The program challenges the able to exercise their minds to complex thinking and achievements. But the program also provides success without prejudice to other students whose talents and motivations are more limited.

MORE RECENT INITIATIVES

The LECI, the MSP's limited and independent follow-up in the western states/provinces of the United States and Canada, retained much of the curricular structure of the earlier project, but gradually expanded its own framework to include a wide range of personalized approaches to curriculum and instruction. The LEC model of personalized education, while focused primarily on instructional process, did encourage its schools to embrace other contemporary programs that emphasized thoughtful reflection, in-depth exploration, and student initiative. The consortium, for example, advocates the concept of "authentic pedagogy" developed by the University of Wisconsin Center on the Reorganization and Restructuring of Schools (see Keefe & Jenkins, 2000; Newmann, Secada, & Wehlage, 1995). CORS defines authentic human achievement in terms of three criteria:

1. Construction of Knowledge—Students are asked to *produce* something, not merely regurgitate what they have heard teachers or other adults say about something. Students must produce real compositions or presentations, perform in plays or sporting events, use technology or machinery, develop functional projects, etc.
2. Disciplined Inquiry—Students build personal knowledge using prior knowledge bases, seek in-depth understanding of a problem, use well thought-out communications to express themselves, and build on their knowledge and skill to understand and solve *new* problems.
3. Value Beyond School—Adult achievement is utilitarian or helpful to others in some way. Student achievement must have value beyond school grades or rank-in-class or scholarships. It must have real-life meaning.

These criteria move the school curriculum in a different direction, beyond simple facts to be memorized, toward what is meaningful for real life. For instance, CORS staff gave an account of fourth- and fifth-grade students doing the measurements, using fractions, and drawing diagrams to design a stereo cabinet. They watched eighth-grade students hold a discussion and construct persuasive arguments about the United States participation in the Vietnam War. They recounted how high school students used geometry to design and create a scale drawing of packaging for soup or cereal containers and then write a short explanation and report how they did it (Newmann et al., 1995).

> The CES is another contemporary alliance of schools that expects them to focus on helping young people to use their minds well. . . . The school's goals should be simple: that each student masters a limited number of essential skills and areas of knowledge. While these skills and areas will, to varying degrees, reflect the traditional academic disciplines, the program's design should be shaped by the intellectual and imaginative powers and competencies that the students need, rather than by "subjects" as conventionally defined. The aphorism "less is more" should dominate: curricular decisions should be guided by the aim of thorough student mastery and achievement rather than by an effort to merely cover content. (CES National Website, 2002a)

A recent example of this kind of personalized education is Harlem's Central Park East Secondary School (CPE), a member of the CES. CPE is actually four schools in one. The majority of the students are African American or Latino and poor (Meier, 1995, p. 16). A central tenet of CPE is described by David Bensman (2000):

> CPE begins not with what outside experts have predetermined that the students need to learn, but with the students' own ideas and interests. The staff listen carefully to what children are saying and observe what they are doing. But most important, they respect those thoughts and actions. (p. 2)

The basic idea of *respecting* the integrity of the students was the touchstone to tapping the energy level of the students in the educational process. It also linked students and their parents to CPE and became the "core" of the teacher-student relationship. The success of CPE has been remarkable. Of the first seven graduating elementary classes, 85% received regular diplomas compared to only 50% citywide. Fewer than 5% who enrolled in CPE at the ninth grade dropped out of the school. Ninety percent of the graduates go on to college.

Alice Seletsky (2000), a longtime teacher at CPE commented further:

> Another belief about teaching and learning was that one had to know what a youngster cared about in order to support and sustain that interest in the classroom. The challenge was greatest with children who showed little interest in the activities available or the possibilities we suggested. (p. 134)

The cornerstone of CPE was this fundamental respect for the student and his/her interest in something that could become the linchpin for other things. Teachers knew they had to find out what this was for each student. Conversely, the use of tests to improve education, to replace man as the measure of all things with the measurement of all things, is a tragedy, despite its political appeal. Deborah Meier (2002) said it best:

> Adopting such a system [a curriculum devoid of children's interests] means that many a curriculum related to children's interests or contemporary or spontaneous events must be ignored. (pp. 195–196)

And the idea that such an instrument [a test] should define our necessarily varied, and at times, conflicting definitions of being well educated
is—worse still—undesirable. (p. 192)

CES schools formulate their curricula based on what students can "exhibit." Exhibitions drive their program planning. But what kind of curriculum does this assessment generate? In *Horace's School,* Theodore Sizer (1992) has his fictitious teacher-hero ponder, "What familiar disciplines are represented in [this school's] list of Exhibitions?" Horace answers himself that four areas are represented: (a) communications and forms of inquiry; (b) mathematics and science; (c) the arts, including literature; and (d) history and philosophy. (The curricular domains in the Francis W. Parker Charter Essential School, co-founded with others by Sizer and his wife Nancy, are Arts and Humanities including the Spanish language, Mathematics, Science and Technology, and Health and Adventure; see the Parker School website.) Sizer goes on to state that "the pedagogical challenge . . . is to tailor the material to our particular kids—without cheapening it. The skills and knowledge implicit in these exhibitions and what lies behind them are fundamentals for *all citizens*" (Sizer, 1992, pp. 109–110). But elsewhere Sizer cautions that "We have learned that nothing is more difficult for essential school people than this work with exhibitions. It demands thinking about learning and the curriculum and teaching and assessment differently from the ways in which most of us were trained" (Sizer, 1996).

ESSENTIAL LEARNING: HIGH STAKES OR INTELLECTUAL TARGETS?

No state accountability plan can ultimately be successful if learners are not considered the most important part of the approach. It may be possible to devise assessments that are uniform for the *essential* aspects of the curriculum, but the selection of evaluative tools must become much more flexible for the *desirable* and *quest* parts of any curriculum. Instead of insisting on across-the-board standardization of student learning, the states may have to settle for a broad band of assessment approaches including curriculum-referenced tests, student portfolios, demonstrations, or exhibitions. The lack of absolute comparability may bother the politicians who want information primarily for more accurate ratings of schools. This political requirement has to be balanced against the need for real intellectual targets that are important to individual students. Student learning must be the centerpiece of educational accountability.

The MSP made curricular and instructional renewal a high priority. Its director, J. Lloyd Trump, argued for continuous student contact with all areas of human knowledge, more time for student special talents and interests, the use of materials permitting student continuous progress, adoption of content more related to the real world, and more utilization of community resources in learning. The MSP basic curriculum incorporated what was *essential* for all students, with other experiences for the more motivated and/or talented. The creators of the project hoped that students would come to see learning as a part of their daily lives rather than just a requirement of schooling. The MSP curriculum was individualized, and self-pacing and mastery-based. The concept of a curriculum focused on essential learning, but with responsible flexibility and accountability, has persisted in the LEC model, in the performance and real-world orientation of CORS authentic pedagogy, and especially in the exhibition-based curricula of the CES.

The MSP, LEC, and CES emphasized the importance of the whole program—the *gestalt of schooling.* It is clear to those of us who have watched the undulating phases of school renewal and reform over the years that nothing lasting can be achieved without this perspective. Moreover, any notion of "school quality" that does not take into account student motivation based on at least some form of choice in the curriculum is unlikely to mean very much to students, even if it is cheap. And any educational system that alienates students, parents, and teachers will ultimately be corrosive of both the means and the ends of schooling in a democratic society.

We clearly need to take some steps back from a condition of over-regulation and over-specification in which heavy-handed mandates drive out all possibility of student interest as well as any salutary educational change and reform. Much of contemporary state testing is antithetical to Western cultural values despite the appearance of concern for "essential learning." The aim of education should be increased humanity and human development, not an input-process-output "black box" that is grounded in the tools of measurement and indices of cost-effectiveness. We seem today to be engaged not only in de-education, but also in the alienation of students and teachers at the lowest possible cost. Recognizing where we have come is the first step toward reversing a direction that is both anti-intellectual and contrary to Western cultural traditions. Before we can move toward personalizing curriculum and instruction on any larger scale, we must work to reverse the tide of regulation that has made that desirable goal all but impossible. We could hardly do better than to look to the MSP for a starting point.

CHAPTER 7

Individualized to Personalized Instruction

John M. Jenkins

Personalized instruction is more than being able to call students by their first names. It is also more than an individualized approach to instruction that allows students to progress at their own pace. It seems best described as a process of designing schoolwork that engages both the attention and the commitment of students. Such a process calls for knowing students better than they know themselves and convincing them through activity and experiences that what they are asked to do in school will add value to their lives, increase their level of essential knowledge, and improve their decision-making skills. It also calls for holding students accountable for their decisions and helping them change direction when the choices are inappropriate.

The history of education is replete with attempts to make learning more personal. From the image of Mark Hopkins, the teacher, seated on one end of a log and James Garfield, his student, seated on the other end to programmed instruction and computer-assisted instruction, the search has been one of looking for ways to consider individual differences in delivering instruction. But the focus of this historical search may have been obvious from the outset. Namely, learning has always been and always will be a personal matter. The meaning that individuals derive from information is colored by their variety and depth of experience. No matter how diligently efforts to mass-produce education have been undertaken, the fact remains that when information impacts an individual, the individual's personal history, previous learning, and preference for learning in a particular way determine the meaning he or she derives.

Perhaps in light of new insights and new research findings, especially in the cognitive sciences, more educators are beginning to realize that personalized learning is inevitable. Combining personalized instruction with personalized learning seems a logical and powerful step for improving schools and for ensuring success for all students.

Keefe (1989) defines personalized education as "a systematic effort on the part of a school to take into account individual student characteristics and effective instructional practices in organizing the learning environment." Carroll (1975) calls it

> an attempt to achieve a balance between the characteristics of the learner and the learning environment. It is the match of the learning environment with the learner's information processing strategies, concepts, learning sets, motivational systems achieved, and skills acquired. It is a continual process.

Personalized instruction extends this definition by giving prominence to the interaction and thoughtfulness of the process.

THE LESSONS OF THE MODEL SCHOOLS PROJECT

The NASSP MSP scheduled students into large group, small group, and independent or supervised study arrangements. The curriculum was divided into eight areas of knowledge: English-language arts; social studies; mathematics; science; other cultures; health, recreation, and fitness; the fine arts; and the practical arts. A ninth area, religion, was added in parochial schools. Students scheduled a large group instruction session, with approximately 100 students, in each of the eight areas once every two weeks. The large group sessions were predominantly motivational and focused on helping students see the value of pursuing the subject in greater depth. Large group sessions were followed by small group reaction sessions of 15 or 20 students to clarify the content presented in the large group. The heart of the MSP instructional program, however, was independent or supervised study. It was in this setting that students pursued learning for academic credit toward graduation. They devoted at least 60% of their school week to independent pursuits.

To facilitate IS, teachers created learning packages and supervised students working alone or in small groups. The learning packages were developed in each of the eight areas of the curriculum and focused on helping students meet the objectives of the curricula. Their teacher-advisers, whose responsibility was to know them as "total human beings" educationally and to guide and monitor their academic progress, scheduled the students into subject areas. With the help of their advisers, students chose to devote more or less time to the completion of work in different subject areas. The IS time was controlled by the advisers and could be altered on a daily basis. The framework for this form of individualized instruction was a cycle of diagnosis, prescription, implementation, and evaluation (DPIE). (See Figure 7.1.)

Students were pre-tested over the objectives of the learning package. If they passed the pre-test, they were then given the post-test. Successful completion of both the pre- and post-test resulted in granting credit

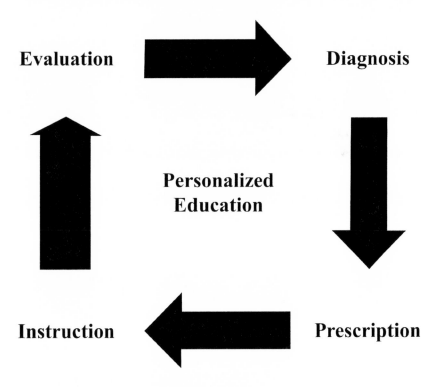

Figure 7.1.   *Framework for Individualized Instruction*

for completing the package. Learning packages were keyed to scope and sequences for each course. When students successfully completed all the components of the scope and sequence, they were granted credit for the course. Using this approach, students were able to progress at their own rate, taking end-of-unit tests when they were ready rather than by the traditional approach of testing everyone on the same day.

Ideally, the learning packages contained various ways for students to complete the objectives. The model acknowledged that certain students learn better by viewing, seeing, or touching than by reading or listening, while other students prefer to read. Teachers diagnosed students' needs and helped each one find the materials that was best for him or her. The model emphasized alternatives for students, but in most cases, the students completed similar activities. Both the teacher-adviser and the subject area team monitored student progress. When a student's progress was judged inadequate, a conference was held to help him/her write a plan to address the problem.

The methodology of DPIE was cyclical. The *diagnosis* led to an appropriate *prescription*—working alone, helping another student or being helped, working with a group on a project, attending a special interest group to listen to a presentation, or to discuss a topic, or for special remedial or advanced work. *Prescriptions* led to *implementation* of instruction. The final step was *evaluation,* to determine the success of the prescription and implementation in terms of student learning. Evaluation then led to further diagnosis and the cycle began anew.

THE THOMAS HANEY APPROACH

The LEC adopted Keefe's extension of the DPIE model (Keefe, 1989). Keefe's elaboration includes three subsections under each of the major headings as shown in Figure 7.2. LEC advocates this model because research and practice show its high correlation with student achievement.

In the early 1990s, LEC personnel worked closely with the Superintendent Denis Therrien and his staff in the Maple Ridge/Pitt Meadows School District #42, Maple Ridge, British Columbia, to plan for the opening of a new secondary school to meet the expanding student pop-

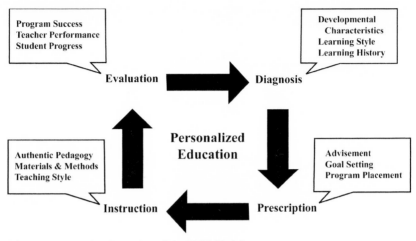

Figure 7.2. *Keefe's Extension of the DPIE Model*

ulation. The superintendent viewed the opening of a new school as an opportunity to do something different. The plan incorporated all the components of Keefe's expanded personalized education model. The educational specifications led to the physical specifications for a new building with open spaces, seminar areas, laboratories, and common planning areas for the faculty.

At Thomas Haney School in Maple Ridge, students meet daily with their teacher-advisers to plan their days. Using a school-developed planner, each student develops his/her agenda. Agendas are usually completed for a week, approved by the student's adviser, and subject to change based upon student needs. The diagnostic component of the DPIE model includes administration of the *Learning Style Profile*, a research-based instrument that reports student strengths, preferences, and limitations on 24 discrete learning style elements. The results for individual students are interpreted, collated, and used to develop alternate pathways to common objectives.

The Ministry of Education for the Province of British Columbia defines the curriculum for courses taught at Haney. Each course is further defined at the school level in terms of units called *learning guides,* written by teams of teachers. Each learning guide represents 1/20th of a course. In each learning guide students will find expectations, learning outcomes, needed resources, and evaluation strategies. Guides are constantly changing and evolving to enable them to remain current, relevant, and student-friendly. The school has developed the following directions for preparing the guides:

- Directions should be brief, clearly stated, and at a suitable reading level.
- Activities should be varied to accommodate different learning styles and contain an approximate time frame for completion.
- Outcomes should be clearly stated and accompanied by quality exemplars to demonstrate completed expectations.
- Final evaluation should incorporate alternative means of assessment for meeting the outcomes, in addition to paper and pencil tests.
- A procedure should be provided to enable students to gain credit for what they already know.

There is no master timetable that students or teachers are obligated to follow each school day. Every student at Thomas Haney has a personalized daily schedule that is planned for his or her specific educational needs. These personal schedules may be changed at any time the needs, interests, or circumstances of the student change. The student's goals for the day/week/month are determined through a collaborative team approach involving the student, parents, and teacher-adviser.

This personalized process is facilitated by the use of a continuous progress approach to scheduling. Most of the students' time is devoted to independent, paired, or team learning on the various activities in the subject-matter learning guides. These activities are augmented by larger group activities scheduled by teachers as needed or in courses that require group activities to be successful, for example, band, chorus, and team sports.

Each student is assigned a teacher-marker in each subject area. This person evaluates all student work and is the student's contact person for the course. Teacher schedules are posted throughout the school to assist students in locating their teacher-markers at any given time. The learning guides facilitate students moving at their own reasonable pace, choosing a time to write tests, and presenting other forms of work for assessment when ready. The continuous progress schedule allows students to have multiple entry points into courses and programs. With the student, teacher-adviser, and parent in control, students have the opportunity to master concepts, skills, and objectives in concert with their unique needs and work habits.

The school has attempted to meet the individual interests of students by offering cross-curricular programs such as the integrated studies program in grade 9 (English, mathematics, science, and social studies) and the Community Studies project in grade 11 (biology, social studies, earth science, physical education, and work experience). Additionally, students are strongly encouraged to negotiate credits for more than one learning guide by getting involved in activities that touch more than one subject area, for example, physical education for a biology field trip to a logging site. Community projects are available to the students with the "signoffs" by appropriate personnel.

The role of the teacher-adviser is significant and crucial to the school's quest to personalize learning. Advisers monitor the behavior, attendance, and academic progress of 20–22 students. They serve as educational consultants, motivators, mentors, coaches, and cheerleaders for their advisees. Advisers assist advisees with educational planning and provide personalized feedback to parents. The students meet with their teacher-advisers for one hour every Monday morning and for 15 minutes at the start of the other four days. On Thursdays, there is a flexible 45-minute time period scheduled to allow advisers to confer with advisees on an individual basis.

The results of an action research study conducted by the Thomas Haney School administration and staff revealed that successful students at Haney exhibit the following characteristics and behavior traits:

- Attend daily and on time.
- Have a daily and weekly plan—use their *Planner* wisely.
- Know what work is expected and check completion daily.
- Communicate with their teacher-markers every two days minimally.
- Attend after-school sessions if work is not done.
- Know the teacher-marker's schedule in each subject taken for credit.
- Work on a maximum of four courses each day.

- Choose compatible work partners.
- Take the necessary resources to the work areas.
- Minimize their movement during the day.
- Use the time in the work areas productively.

Working with their advisers and with the support of their parents, most, if not all, Haney students internalize these behaviors.

Parents are expected to work with their student, the teacher-adviser, and the teaching staff to create a learning environment where student success is the primary goal. Responsibilities of the parents include involvement in goal setting, planning, ensuring regular attendance, and monitoring the completion of learning guides. *The Parents' Guide*, a publication of the school, lists the following tasks for each parent:

- Initiate and maintain regular contact with the teacher-adviser.
- Observe how your child learns best and communicate this information to the teacher-adviser.
- Monitor your child's rate of progress.
- Review your child's *Planner* and note the schedule he or she is following.
- Review and check the student learning guide completion pages and the monthly progress report found in the *Planner*.
- Get all progress updates, report cards, and attend parent-teacher days.
- Help your child take ownership of his or her education.
- Be a spokesperson in the community for the positive things that occur in the school.

Personalizing instruction at Haney is an integral part of the school's culture. All stakeholders perceive their role as one of support for individual learners as they pursue their studies and discover their unique talents. In their book *Personalized Instruction*, Keefe and Jenkins (2000) identify six basic elements of personalized instruction: (a) dual teacher role of coach and adviser, (b) the diagnosis of relevant student characteristics, (c) a collegial school culture, (d) an interactive learning environment, (e) flexible scheduling and pacing, and (f) authentic assessment. It appears that the program at Thomas Haney meets each one.

A STEP BEYOND

Keefe and Jenkins (2000) further describe personalized instruction by elaborating on the dimension of interaction and introducing the idea of thoughtfulness. Interaction refers to the degree of involvement between the student and the teachers, the student and other students, and the student and instructional materials. Thoughtfulness relates to the depth of the material a student engages, the amount of reflection generated, and the degree of understanding that results. Keefe and Jenkins rate 20 different instructional approaches on a two-dimensional matrix. Four approaches were rated highest on both interaction and thoughtfulness.

It appears a common misconception among many educators desiring to personalize instruction that some means of self-pacing is necessary, and that group activities of any kind are antithetical to true personalization. According to Keefe and Jenkins (2000), this is not necessarily the case. Of the four highest-rated approaches, only guided practice could ostensibly qualify as a type of self-pacing. A brief description of the top four personalized instruction approaches follows. Readers interested in a more thorough description of each approach are advised to consult Keefe and Jenkins's *Personalized Instruction*, chapter 5.

Topic Study (Storyline): Topic study, or storyline, originated in Scotland and is a product of the Jordanhill College of Education. Originally developed for students at the elementary level, it is now available for middle-level students and awaits only the creative effort of a high school educator to accommodate that level of schooling. As the term *storyline* implies, the approach centers on a story of real interest to a classroom of students. For example, one storyline episode began with the teacher drafting a letter from the National Aeronautics and Space Administration (NASA) to his class challenging them to create a space station capable of sustaining human life. Once the students accepted the challenge, they were off and running as participants in their own learning. A class-created mural established the context in which the challenge took place and identified roles important to the various tasks necessary to meet the challenge.

Topic study focuses on a theme and usually requires an extended period to complete. The thematic approach integrates subject matter—reading, writing, spelling, mathematics, science, social studies, literature, and the expressive arts. In many elementary schools, storyline does not take the place of regular instruction, but rather is scheduled in blocks two to three times per week. Students work directly with primary sources and are guided by the teacher to generate questions that lead to hypotheses, which in turn lead to tentative answers and then to more questions. Traditional classrooms become laboratories, venues for learning, to immerse students in the learning process. Students frequently work in teams where opportunities to learn from each other are plentiful. Teachers employ tactics such as modeling, coaching, and scaffolding to help students understand complex concepts, draw from their own experiences, and posit their own theories.

Cognitive Apprenticeship: Closely aligned with topic study/storyline is the cognitive apprenticeship. Based on the concept of situated learning, the cognitive apprenticeship places students in a rich and varied context that is meaningful and authentic. The method attempts to acculturate students into authentic practices through activity and social interaction in a way similar to the craft apprenticeships (Brown, Collins, & Duguid, 1989). Historically, the craft apprenticeship was the way in which formal knowledge was transmitted, whether the field was law, medicine, the arts, or a myriad of crafts. In his biography of President John Adams, David McCullough (2001) recounts Adams' experience as a young apprentice in a law office in Massachusetts studying to become a lawyer.

Cognitive apprenticeships seek to engage learners in real-world scenarios in which they act and interact to achieve useful outcomes. They follow a framework that includes several types of content, various instructional methods, a sequencing of tasks, and an appropriate setting. Brill, Kim, and Galloway (2001) juxtapose fourth-grade classrooms, one using a traditional approach and one employing a cognitive apprenticeship approach. Both classrooms are focused on the Great Depression as the content. The traditional classroom uses a textbook approach with didactic instruction. It is well managed but basically passive with regard to student involvement. In the cognitive apprenticeship classroom students interact with three community consultants who lived through the Great Depression. The consultants share mementos, photographs, and other items from the era. Working in teams, students prepare specific questions for interviewing the consultants. Each student conducts an interview session with one of the consultants. Records are kept using camcorders, digital cameras, and journal entries. The teacher guides small groups of students to consider certain questions, organize their thoughts, and consult a variety of resources, including books, videos, the Internet, and other people. The culminating class project is a multimedia presentation documenting the Great Depression from a local perspective, "Life in Our Community During the Great Depression." It is presented at the town library on Memorial Day.

The cognitive apprenticeship is a recursive process, usually beginning with some form of modeling by teachers, experts, or peers. Support is provided for students' guided practice using scaffolding and coaching. Supports are withdrawn based on the teacher's assessment of an individual student's ability to function independently, all the time revisiting what he or she has done and discussing his or her ideas with other students and the teacher. The final products of individuals, groups, or the total class become grist for analysis, reflection, evaluation, and future planning.

For a high school example of a cognitive apprenticeship, the film "October Sky" describes a science fair project conducted by several high school students in West Virginia as a response to the Russian launching of Sputnik in 1957. Fenwick English's (1989) description of a school for the year 2088, where students are immersed in authentic venues of historical time zones, also qualifies as a high school example.

Guided Practice: This form of pedagogy is widely used in athletics and the arts. Coaches demonstrate what they want players or performers to do and then observe them carefully as they attempt to do it. The performance becomes the assessment, which is rated in terms of an optimal performance. Corrections are made, the performance is repeated, and a second evaluation is made. The process continues until the performance approximates the standard.

In a classroom setting, the student practices a target behavior under the supervision of a teacher-coach. The practice may extend over a period of time, with the teacher asking appropriate questions to gain insight so as to help optimize the student's behavior. The "performance" could be a problem-solving strategy, a subject-matter discipline or skill, or a presentation before the class. The teacher may even ask the students to verbalize the steps they are using, in a form of metacognition.

The feedback is actually a formative-type assessment that leads the teacher to suggest subsequent steps. The coaching model may be used with an individual student, a small group, or a class of 25–30 students.

Teacher-coaches provide various kinds of supports to students through didactic instruction, modeling, and skillful questioning. The teacher supports are adjusted in accordance with individual student learning characteristics, the nature of the task, and the nature of the material. They are removed gradually as the students demonstrate an ability to function independently.

Cooperative Learning: Of the four highest-rated approaches to personalized instruction, cooperative learning is perhaps the best known and the most widely implemented. It was made popular by the seminal work of David and Roger Johnson at the University of Minnesota and Robert Slavin at Johns Hopkins University. In William Glasser's (1990) book, *The Quality School*, he recommends that 75% of classroom instruction utilize some form of cooperative learning. He bases this recommendation on the amount and degree of interaction among students and the degree of engagement encouraged by the process.

Cooperative learning groups are usually five to seven students working together to accomplish an academic task. Each student is held accountable for both successfully completing the academic task and nurturing the working relationships within the group. The teacher's role is to establish the task and procedure, encourage interdependency among the group members, provide resources or suggest resources, and monitor progress.

Four elements are essential to the group's success: (a) positive interdependence among the learners, (b) face-to-face interaction, (c) individual and group accountability, and (d) adequate interpersonal skills. The following strategies are a sample of the kinds of cooperative group endeavors available to teachers in planning engaging work for students. In each case, clear task definition and direction is paramount.

- *Student Teams-Achievement Division (STAD)*: Students are heterogeneously grouped in five-member teams. The teacher introduces new material didactically or by class discussion. The students work together to complete worksheets or assignments keyed to the content. Assessments are completed individually.

- *Teams, Games, and Tournaments (TGT)*: This strategy uses the same team, instructional format, and assignment sheets as STAD. Students participate in weekly academic tournaments to demonstrate their mastery of content. Competition is organized among equally achieving students representative of different teams. Individual student scores contribute to the team score in judging the results of the competition.
- *Jigsaw*: Students are assigned to six-member teams to pursue content arranged in five related sections (two students share one of the sections). Each student investigates his or her section carefully to become the "expert" for his/her team. Cross-team "expert" groups meet to share findings on the same section. Assessment is individualized.
- *Group Investigation of Team Learning*: Five- to seven-member groups use inquiry methods and group discussion to develop a cooperative project as a subset of a larger theme or unit. The subtopics are divided into individual tasks and assigned to specific group members. The final product is a presentation of the groups' findings to the class.

THE VISION OF PERSONALIZED INSTRUCTION

Educators hold many beliefs about how schools should be operated. Beliefs such as "students learn differently" and "the more time students devote to the study of a subject, the more they learn" give rise to a vision or ideal to be realized. Perceived gaps between the vision and the status quo lead to a development of a school mission that, when achieved, will reduce the gaps and bring the ideal closer to fruition.

The ideal of personalizing instruction acknowledges differences among students, the importance of lifelong learning, the value of intrinsic motivation, and learning in context. Transforming the ideal to the real can take several forms, some of which are described in this chapter. Self-paced, self-directed learning gives credence to the belief that time measures only time. It doesn't measure achievement. Advisement programs resonate the message that *all* students are important and that students' personal well-being helps satisfy basic needs.

The contextualized learning of topic study/storyline and cognitive apprenticeships lead more effectively to the transfer of knowledge by helping students learn content and skills at the same time as they apply them in meaningful ways.

Certainly, competency in basic skills is important no matter what a student's ultimate future; however, personalized instruction means much more than providing alternative pathways to common goals. Schools should capitalize on the myriad of ways in which students differ. Designing educational environments to enable students to discover and celebrate their differences seems the business of schools in the twenty-first century. Lifelong learning implies a devotion to actualizing one's unique talents, and school seems a likely place for getting a jump-start on this process. In 1964 at Melbourne High School in Melbourne, Florida (the first non-graded high school in the United States), the master schedule contained the following challenge addressed to each student: "You are the entrepreneur of your own education." More recently, Elliot Eisner (2003), in an article in *The Phi Delta Kappan,* contends that the goal of education should go beyond merely high scores on standardized tests. Eisner argues, "the major aim of schooling is to enable students to become the architects of their own education so that they may invent themselves during the course of their lives." Individualized instruction may initiate the process, but personalized instruction is the appropriate extension. Above the archway of a high school in Pennsylvania is inscribed, "To Teach the Art of Living Well." These words from the Stoic philosopher Seneca seem as timely today as they were when written during the first century in Rome.

CHAPTER 8

Developments in School Culture, Climate, and School Effectiveness

Michael Martin, Eugene R. Howard, and Clifton Colia

"The MSP encouraged school stakeholders to improve the 'ethos' of schooling and to provide for each pupil, regardless of talents or interests, a program through which he (or she) may proceed with gains" (Trump & Georgiades, 1970). Following on the MSP, the NASSP, LECI, and the LEC Forum advocated that schools pursue a local, design-based planning process to develop Design Statements that included specifications for the strengthening of school climate and culture. In this chapter we outline the progress that has been made by the educational profession since the time of the MSP in defining and advocating positive school climates and cultures. We discuss the relationships between climate, culture, and school effectiveness, the research and key components of climate and culture, and briefly review the process of involving stakeholders in school design activities that form a school's research-based improvement plan. We close with some challenges in linking school climate, culture, and renewal.

OVERVIEW: THE ANTECEDENTS OF SCHOOL CLIMATE, CULTURE, AND EFFECTIVENESS

For well over a century educators, policymakers, and other citizens have sought better ways to increase student learning, teacher effectiveness, and school improvement. From the pioneering efforts of John Dewey's experimental school in the late 1890s at the University of Chicago (Tanner, 1997) to the more recent No Child Left Behind legislation, many reforms have attempted to strengthen education in America (Keefe &

Jenkins, 2000). Educational improvement has been at the top of the national agenda for the past 40 years and continues to occupy front-page interest (Darling-Hammond, 1993; Tanner & Tanner, 1990).

These reforms have often centered on addressing or eliminating the perception, and often the reality, of public education as characterized by "lockstep" curricula, standardization, "stand and deliver" instruction, bureaucratic management, rigid grading, social promotion, illiterate graduates, and "failing" schools. Interestingly, many of these reform efforts did not originate from within the public schools but were initiated from outside the regular K–12 educational establishment. Leadership came from at least five diverse types of organizations, including American foundations, universities, businesses and community organizations, the federal government, and education-oriented professional organizations. These outside sources demonstrated significant commitment to school reform through their influence, political pressure, funding, and publications.

Three notable efforts form the backdrop for this chapter, and we must acknowledge them as contributing to our own interest and involvement in school improvement since the 1960s:

1. The first initiative was the ground-breaking and successful "Eight-Year Study," which occurred between 1933 and 1941 and was funded by the Progressive Education Association. It investigated alternative paths to college preparatory education and how innovation in education might best occur.
2. The second was the visionary partnership between the Ford and Danforth Foundations and the NASSP, particularly in the years between the 1950s and the 1970s. This partnership spawned the MSP, led to the organization of LEC, and encouraged many other reform movements that occurred in the United States and England.
3. A third effort stemmed from the commitment of the Charles F. Kettering Foundation to school reform through such mechanisms as the League of Cooperating Schools in California, IGE in Wisconsin and Ohio, and the CFK Ltd. initiatives, "conducting school climate improvement projects" in the early 1970s through the 1980s. (Fox et al., 1974; Goodlad, 1975, 1984; Howard, Howell, & Brainard, 1987)

SCHOOL CULTURE, CLIMATE, AND
EFFECTIVENESS: ESSENTIAL LINKS

What is it in the culture and climate of organizations that tends to inhibit the installation of innovations designed to increase school effectiveness? Our experience in school reform has shown that reforms or innovations aimed at improving school effectiveness can rarely be successful if the climate and culture of a school are not seriously considered by school leaders and reformers (Colia, 2001).

School Culture

Scholars often debate the anthropological (Geertz, 1973) and sociological (Dalin, 1973) roots of culture and little consensus exists on a single definition, particularly when leadership and organizational culture are added to the equation (Brown, 1995). There are in fact more than 150 definitions of "culture" in the literature (Ott, 1989), yet there are at least two recurring themes that have implications for education:

1. Culture is the primary means by which participants in a school live and adjust to the issues and problems presented by their dynamic environments.
2. Culture is the sum of the values, ideas, behavior, and products that have been shared, learned, or used by a particular group of school participants as a secure way to control or adapt to their environment. One of the leading scholars of culture, Edgar Schein (1985), states that culture is a uniquely human product, that it must be learned and shared, is in a constant state of change, and is passed on through education, socialization, or acculturation.

Culture is the outcome of "group learning" that solves organizational problems and contains and reduces anxiety for the group (Schein, 1985). Deal (1993) adds specifics to this definition that have dramatic implications for the study of school culture. To him, culture is an "all encompassing tapestry of meaning . . . the way we do things around here . . . (which) includes shared values, heroes, rituals, ceremonies, stofies, and an informal network of cultural sub-groups" (pp. 6–7). From this definition it can be seen that schools have "norms" which are both written and un-written that lead to rules and expectations for student and adult behavior, which in turn exert pressure on members of groups in a school to conform their actions and attitudes to that range which is considered acceptable by the group. If a new group of teachers, for example, is pursuing "personal-ized education" or "project-based learning" and the veteran group op-poses them, the culture of the school in its extreme and worst-case form can enforce the *status quo* over new initiatives.

The Difficulties in Changing School Culture

Many cultural "norms" are unwritten yet provide important stability to school participants through rites, rituals, stories, and sanctions.

Deal suggests that schools must build or rework norms on a regular basis to encourage change if the participants desire it. Every faculty and school community will have its own unique culture that is deeply rooted in tradition and history and has become the "blueprint" for the group's thinking, doing and believing "a road map that gets the group from one day to the next" (Naylor, 1996). This explains why school re-formers such as those in the MSP, LEC, and the CES have had such dif-ficulty installing innovatitions. Schools are imprinted with norms, val-ues, and beliefs that are highly resistant to change because they have helped the school survive the turbulent environment in which it often finds itself—high stakes vs. low stakes testing; back to the basics vs. constructivist learning; lecture vs. project-based education, etc. Schol-ars such as Naylor, Schein, and others are uncertain about the means and patterns of success associated with changing the culture of any or-ganization. The challenge for school leaders is to study, redesign, change, and manage school organizations so that they are more re-sponsive to their stakeholders as they seek greater levels of effective-ness. Schein (1985) argues that "The unique and essential function of leadership is the manipulation of culture."

Cultural and Learning Networks in Schools

The changing emphases on culture are encouraging, as advocated in the literature by such practitioner-oriented scholars as Peter Senge,

Fred Kofman, Rosabeth Moss Kanter, Charles Handy, and others (Chawla & Renesch, 1995). These authors believe that organizations as well as the people in them can learn, and that learning consists of deriving meaning from knowledge and the thoughtful implementation of what is being learned. This suggests, for example, that school leaders, faculty members, and the school community should regularly examine and be aware that the following elements of culture can inhibit or foster school effectiveness: rituals, taboos, myths, ceremonies, celebrations, games, laws, rules, symbols, shared language, assumptions, values, visions and beliefs, and enforcement processes. It is also clear from the work of Deal that each school has a cultural "network" that consists of storytellers, priests, gossips, spies, cabals, heroes, and heroines, among others (Deal, 1982, pp. 87–94).

School leaders should also be aware that scholars have identified numerous "subcultures" in organizations that must be acknowledged if innovation is to be considered. In schools, these can include, among others, jocks, preppies, homeboys, cowboys, ropers, and isolates. One of the lessons learned from the Columbine incident is that these subcultures can be highly destructive of effective relationships among and between students, faculty, administrators, and parents.

Defining School Culture

After examining the history and scholarship of culture, we define school culture as follows: The shared values, beliefs, and norms of an individual school that govern both its behavior and attitudes, and that find expression through the overt and symbolic phenomena of that school community (Deal, 1993; Kilman, Saxton, & Serpa, 1985; Smircich, 1983). In short, "the way we do things around here" (Deal, 1987).

If new approaches are to be effectively considered and installed in schools, leaders must examine the school culture via observations, interviews, artifact collection, and surveys. The key areas for reformers and school leaders to examine either in person or by survey include the following: shared values, school norms, beliefs held by the various school community members, symbols, celebrations, rituals, subcultures, taboos, enforcement mechanisms, ceremonies, rules, and language.

A review of the literature relating school culture to school effective-ness shows that effective schools have cultural values that: (a) value success for all students, (b) hold high expectations for student achieve-ment, (c) hold beliefs in a common vision for what the school should be accomplishing, and (d) cherish the belief that collaboration is nec-essary between members of a school community (Colia, 2001, p. 6). Sarason (1971) also found in his seminal work at Yale on school cul-ture that the underlying beliefs and values of school organizations con-tribute to school effectiveness.

School Climate

As indicated earlier, the MSP cited the importance of the "ethos" of a school to "provide for each pupil, regardless of talents or interests, a program through which he may proceed with gains." The factors that educators have viewed as necessary for student and school success have changed dramatically during the past 30 years, and "climate has been one of those concepts that has been bewildering, confusing and often competitive among scholars and practitioners" (Colia, 2001, pp. 3–5). Climate has been framed in terms of the physical and structural compo-nents of a school, the outcome of both a rigorous and comprehensive curriculum, and the product of a well-defined instructional process.

Secondary school accreditation reinforced this structural aspect of schooling by emphasizing the importance of "measurable" school charac-teristics such as numbers of library books, teacher certification, counselor/ student ratios, and the like. It represented a more "quantitative or exter-nal" view of school quality and, while important, does not account for school or student success. After works produced by such scholars as James Coleman (1966) and Christopher Jencks (1972) began to show that expenditures and other factors such as books, teacher certification, and advising ratios (among other such variables) did not explain much about student achievement, "interpersonal capital" in schools began to receive more attention in the mid-1970s in the dialogue about the rela-tion between climate and school effectiveness (Brookover, 1982; Fox et al., 1974; Howard et al., 1987; Howell & Grahlman, 1978; Hoy & Miskel, 1987; Keefe & Howard, 1997; Moos, 1979; Rutter, 1979).

Defining School Climate

The NASSP Task Force on the School Environment, as cited in Keefe and Howard (1997, p. 24), defined school climate as "the relatively enduring pattern of shared perceptions—by teachers, students, parents, and community members—of the characteristics of a school and of its members." The literature is replete with the elements of climate.

The early work by the Charles Kettering's CFK Ltd. group contributed several dimensions to climate: (a) *Climale Factors,* such as trust, respect, cohesiveness; (b) *Program Determinants,* such as opportunities for active learning and varied learning environments; (c) *Process Determinants,* such as effective communications and teaching-learning strategies, and (d) *Material Determinants,* such as suitability of school plant (Fox et al., 1974).

The NASSP Task Force and CASE-IMS program identified ten key climate areas: teacher-student relationships, security and maintenance, administration, student academic orientation, student behavioral values, guidance, student peer relationships, parent and school relationships, instructional management, and student activities (Howard & Keefe, 1991). The CASE-IMS program addressed the perceived concern that managers and leaders typically do little formal data gathering, with most information collected through conversations with various stakeholder individuals or groups, or from observations and reports—the data is largely informal and verbal. Successful school improvement requires the collection of accurate information about the affective and empirical status of a school in order to diagnose the present situation and to know what improvements are needed. The CASE-IMS is designed to enable school leaders to collect and interpret comprehensive data about the school, including information from students, teachers, parents, and administrators about such important areas as climate, satisfaction, and leadership. All data are carefully validated and normed with two goals in mind: (a) to identify strengths and weaknesses in current school performance, and (b) to help select interventions for school improvement or restructuring.

Other scholars have contributed additional elements or insight to school climate (Brookover, 1982; Colia, 2001; Edmonds, 1986; Fox et al., 1974, Goodlad, 1984; Halpin & Croft, 1962; Hoy & Miskel, 1987; Lezotte,

1990; Martin & Howard, 1998; Moos, 1979; Rutter, 1979; Sizer, 1984). The most recent analysis and synthesis of the research on school climate yielded six ingredients of organizational climate that are present in effective schools (Colia, 2001). These include: (a) Organizational Cohesiveness, (b) Participative Decision Making, (c) Trust, (d) Safety, (e) Collegiality, and (f) Proactive Communication.

Distinction Between Culture and Climate

A clear difference exists in the literature between culture and climate, with culture taking on the dimension of "the way things are done around here," and with climate more focused on the shared but often diverse perceptions and reactions of school/community members to the values, attitudes, beliefs, and norms of a given culture (Keefe & Howard, 1997; Schneider, 1990). Climate is more a psychological construct, in contrast to culture's social foundations, and consists in a participant's interpretation of and response to the work environment based on personal experiences and values (James & McIntyre, 1996). Regardless, both culture and climate must be examined and addressed if a school is to increase its effectiveness. Simply providing more money, books, qualified teachers, time on task, and smaller classes is to ignore a major component of an effective school.

Linking School Improvement, Culture, and Climate

In tandem with the work of Coleman (1966) and Jencks (1972) cited earlier, some scholars have concentrated on other important intangibles in school and student effectiveness. Since 1970, educational researchers have attempted to establish the relationship between school effectiveness and climate and culture (Brookover, 1982; Edmonds, 1986; Goodlad, 1984; Lezotte, 1990; Rutter, 1979). They hoped to demonstrate that the social context, or relationship variables, of an individual school's culture had a marked effect on student achievement and on perceptions of effectiveness. The longitudinal approach, direct observations, and staff/pupil interviews conducted during Rutter's study, among others, pointed out the rich detail needed to understand school learning cultures and climates that could never be gleaned from statistical data alone.

The so-called "effective schools movement" left two main legacies from its explorations into the relationships between climate, culture, and effectiveness:

1. Alternatives to the traditional methods of school improvement beyond examining such tangible aspects of schooling as class size, teacher qualifications, school capacity, or single uses of standardized measures such as test scores.
2. More detailed examination of school relationships, communication patterns, values, beliefs, norms, collegiality, and related climate and culture ingredients.

The process of developing effective schools was viewed as more long term and ongoing, with an emphasis on examining and developing the human resources in the school setting. Seymour Sarason (1971), for example, advocated the systematic study of schools as complex organizations and urged that more needed to be learned about the functioning of schools and school systems.

Redesigning or Designing a School for Improved Effectiveness

A "School Design Statement" contains several basic and systemic indicators leading to the development of clear specifications for school planning, including those for culture and climate analysis, as based on the approach by Keefe and Howard (1997) in *Redesigning Schools for the New Century: A Systems Approach*. The *Basic Design Components* require that a school develop (a) *Mission and Vision Statements* that set forth the purpose and reason for the school's existence, (b) *Culture and Climate Statements* that paint a portrait of what a school's norms and values are and how people are responding to them, and (c) *Student Goals and Outcomes Statements*, which identify what is to be learned and the results of that learning.

The *Systemic Design Components* require that a school review and assess: (a) *Curriculum and Instructional Practices*, which include what is taught and how it is taught; (b) *Instructional Strategies*, which address the models of pedagogy and learning; (c) *School Structure and Organization*, which is detailed to ensure synchronization with the goals and outcome statements in the Basic Components; (d) *Leadership and Management* components such as the role of the leader, the management team, how the school is managed at all levels, etc.; (e) *Budgeting and School Resources*, including how funds are planned, supervised, and expended in relation to the mission, vision, goals, and priorities of the school; (f) *Staffing and Staff Development* to ensure that the school goals and outcomes may be accomplished and that school participants have the training necessary to lead and operate an effective school; (g) *Communication and Political Structures,* which assure that all school stakeholders are regularly informed and appropriately involved in the governance of the school; (h) *Physical Plant,* which assures that the school buildings are attractive and efficiently maintained; and (i) *An Evaluation Plan,* which appraises all the components of the design as well as other formative and summative elements. Note that all of these Systemic Design Components relate to a school's culture and climate.

SPECIFIC CONTRIBUTIONS TO CLIMATE AND CULTURE IMPROVEMENT

The MSP achieved varying degrees of success. The LECI was formed in 1974 to carry on the principles of the MSP. LEC is committed to the principle that "piecemeal implementation" of school reform does not work, that change must be comprehensive, and that this change must address culture and climate if substantial and lasting school reform is to occur. During the past 30 years, NASSP, LECI, and its LEC Forum, as well as the CES, have created and/or substantially introduced innovative processes and practices that have had, and will continue to have, positive influence on educational practice. Several of these structures, practices, and procedures have evolved more slowly than anticipated and have had minimal effects on common practice. Some examples are listed below that illustrate these trends and their relationship to culture/climate improvement.

Restructuring

Models for restructuring schools, advocated by the MSP and further developed by LECI and its Forum, substantially changed the culture of schools by providing new environments and learning activities, including independent study, small group discussions, active learning, team teaching (including interdisciplinary teams), technology use, and the matching of teaching styles to learning styles. Flexible scheduling increased access of students to the environments most appropriate to their activities. These designs also contributed and still contribute to teacher and student climate by increasing successful learning experiences for students and by enabling teachers to stimulate learning in a variety of learning environments.

While the restructuring of school learning environments has occurred in many schools, the conventional classroom still predominates and the teacher lecture/student recitation "lockstep" method persists. Time in most schools is still controlled by a rigid schedule and by clock-and-bell systems.

Differentiated Staffing

Early in the process of conceptualizing the needed changes in school environments, Lloyd Trump, Bill Georgiades, Jim Keefe, and other leaders realized that the roles of staff members would have to change if comprehensive change were to result. Various types of teacher assistants were defined and advocated and the role of the principal as instructional leader was redefined and emphasized. Comprehensive change became manageable and "the way we do things around here." (Deal, 1993) was focused on climate improvement and cultural consitency as defined in school design statements. Teachers especially saw differentiated staffing as improving a school's climate.

This practice has evolved in the past 30 years, but not to the extent that we had originally expected. Teacher assistants are available more often in elementary schools and infrequently in secondary institutions. Middle and high school teachers now find themselves progressively overloaded with nonprofessional duties. Budgetary restrictions have impeded progress.

Teacher-Advisement

Programs designed to personalize learning rely on teacher-advisers working with individual students and small groups of students. Components of such programs related to school climate and culture include the development of personalized education plans for each learner and close communication among learners, teachers, parents, and community resource persons. Teacher-advisement programs contribute to school climate improvement by increasing the involvement of students and parents in the decision-making processes. Student self-understanding is likewise enhanced (see Jenkins & Daniel, 2000).

Advisement programs have grown and improved as anticipated, especially in middle-level schools. Their effectiveness, however, has been limited by inadequate staff development and staffing restrictions in schools.

School Design and Redesign Processes

A well-defined process for implementing comprehensive, research-based change was designed, field tested, and demonstrated under NASSP auspices with close LEC collaboration (Howard & Keefe, 1991). The process is based on the belief that widespread involvement in any change process is a necessary component of a school's cultural and climate improvement and ultimately of a school's effectiveness. Progress in school renewal and redesign has been made over the past 30 years and documented in many schools. Change processes have been refined to be more efficient and effective. Design-based change, however, is largely limited to schools with pervasive problems, to alternative schools and charter schools, and to schools with dedicated, highly-committed leaders and faculty. Few schools can display complete design statements which include specifications of the desired culture and characteristics of the desired climate.

Prior to the introduction of the CASE-IMS, the acceptable strategy for improving schools was "piecemeal." CASE-IMS provided leaders with the essential information to guide systemwide change. Specifically targeted for change were "climate" and its related component, "satisfaction." *The CASE-IMS validated "climate" as a key mediating variable of the school environment essential to a comprehensive change process.* One result of this substantial effort was an increased emphasis on climate improvement in school-improvement planning and implementation (see Howard & Keefe, 1991). Nevertheless, even in the face of this improved technology, the problems-centered, piecemeal approach to school improvement still persists.

The Learning Laboratory and Expanded Resource Center

Traditionally, elementary and secondary schools housed learning materials almost exclusively in centralized libraries and classrooms. "Laboratories" were limited to science, industrial arts, fine arts, and home economics. The MSP advocated the use of learning laboratories for all subjects, thereby increasing the variety of learning materials and human resources available to learners. Continuous progress programs and student-initiated activities became more feasible. At least some students could learn at their own rate, develop real research skills, and engage in computer-based activities. (Distance Learning was another consequence of this expanded approach to learning resources.) The culture of schools using learning laboratories was modified from one based on the belief that learning is best facilitated in the traditional classroom and should be teacher-directed. A positive climate is more likely to develop when students are provided with more choices in their own learning activities.

During the past 30 years, learning laboratories and expanded resource centers have been gradually accepted in our elementary and secondary schools. Advancements in various forms of technology, especially computer technology, have enabled such facilities to encourage student-initiated instruction and learning style-based instruction. Continuous progress curricula, however, have been difficult to implement and manage. (Thomas Haney Secondary Centre in British Columbia and Bishop Carroll High School in Alberta, Canada are notable exceptions.)

Authentic Assessment and Progress Reporting

Through the efforts of the CES and LECI, the process of evaluating student achievement in terms of performance on defined objectives is taking on increasing importance. The use of portfolios and demonstrations—"performance assessment"—is emphasized so that learning objectives can be verified. Student self-evaluation is incorporated as a key motivational component. Such a system accentuates the value of lifelong learning skills, a key component of a responsive culture. It also enhances student perceptions of climate by encouraging meaningful student involvement in planning and evaluating the agreed-upon learning objectives.

Acceptance of authentic assessment has been slow but steady. The use of portfolios and learner demonstrations ("exhibitions") is becoming more common. Conventional grading and letter grades (including failing grades) are still dominant. Such grading and ranking practices can have a negative affect on students' perception of self and ultimately on school climate.

Interdisciplinary Teaching and Learning

Interdisciplinary techniques are difficult to implement in traditional secondary schools in which the faculty is organized into subject-matter departments. Newly designed schools usually find it easier to interrelate more than one discipline in lesson plans and presentations. Contemporary change in the basic definition of knowledge has enabled teachers to focus learning on pieces of reality, which are generally interdisciplinary. This is a cultural shift that has the potential of improving instruction and positively influencing school climate.

The practice of interdisciplinary teaching has plateaued during the past three decades. Strict departmentalization of secondary school teaching staffs and single-discipline standardized testing are still the norm. Interdisciplinary teams of teachers are formed, but typically only for special projects. Team-taught large group instruction and team-built curricular units persist, but overall progress seems to be very limited. Small group discussion is somewhat more common, but surely not yet the norm. The emphasis on single-subject teaching persists in spite of new research that shows how learning for meaning and understanding takes place.

CHALLENGES TO SCHOOL CLIMATE, CULTURE, AND RENEWAL

"An academically effective school is distinguished by its culture: a structure, process and climate of values and norms that channel staff and students in the direction of successful learning" (Purkey & Smith, 1982, pp. 64–69). Continual challenges to school culture and climate exist in this era of the standardized test. Standardized testing offers only a "snapshot" of a school on any given day in comparison to the comprehensive picture an assessment process such as CASE-IMS can provide, especially if it is part of a School Design and Improvement process. With advances in technology, cultural renewal and climate improvement become easier to manage. Complex data and design tools for school and instructional improvement are available. Electronic portfolios and computerized databases mean that we can now more easily design continuous progress programs for individual students, judge student mastery more readily, and help learners to manage their own learning more efficiently. Teacher-student advising and mentoring relationships can be more easily monitored with databases so readily available.

Linking learning and effectiveness with educational standards and curriculum is now possible with the aid of technology. Complex communications can now be easily initiated and maintained through technology. Self-paced instruction is already a reality through online learning programs. Personalized learning plans can be created and easily monitored by students and parents. Even greater student-parent involvement can be achieved through advances in technology. Distance learning makes worldwide learning environments more readily available to all students. Research on the complexities of the learning process is becoming more accessible and instructional strategies are being modified accordingly. All of these educational processes, to the extent that they are implemented, can improve a school's cultural cohesiveness and result in improved school climate.

Whatever the future holds for education, a quality school must be created, maintained, and nurtured if students are to learn successfully. Research-compatible design statements, feasible school improvement plans, dedicated design teams, continuous stakeholder collaboration, and constructive results-monitoring will always be key elements in the school of the future. But it all starts with culture and climate. Nothing of enduring value will be accomplished unless schools foster healthy links between school climate, culture, and effectiveness. The MSP argued for a healthy school ethos. Time and research have served to validate that affirmation.

CHAPTER 9

Evaluation and Grading

James W. Keefe

J. Lloyd Trump, director of the NASSP MSP, believed that one of the major imperatives for improving the quality of teaching and learning was to change the process of evaluation (Trump, 1966). He felt that three current practices needed to be abandoned immediately: oral quizzes/classroom discussion, multi-purpose letter grades, and comparison of individual pupils in groups (grading on a curve, class ranks). Trump believed that oral quizzes, recitation, and so-called classroom discussion are a waste of time and highly inefficient ways to discover what learners really know. In these activities, most of the class remains passive while one student is grilled. Similarly, letter grades such as A, B, C, D, F, and their equivalents are useless because they are subjective and provide little real information about a student's work. Comparative grading, in turn, is dependent on the quality of a given group and can give some students (and their parents) a false sense of superiority while other students always end up at the bottom of the ranking no matter how competent objectively they may be. Trump (1966) urged that

> a first step in replacing these three practices is to identify and to describe the goals that teachers seek for pupils. One of these goals is to grow in knowledge and skills. . . . If the teacher needs to check on growth in discussion skills, this is easy to do. The teacher sitting in as the observer and critic keeps a tally of how often the students participate in the discussion and the quality of what they say. . . . The point is that matters such as IS, oral discussion skills, habits of inquiry, interpersonal relations are reported to parents and to students, to colleges and employers, along with achievements in knowledge and skills.

MODEL SCHOOLS PROJECT

J. Lloyd Trump carried this view of evaluation and grading, with a few modifications, to the MSP three years later. He proposed that the "schools of tomorrow" should be allowed to develop more valid ways of judging educational excellence. The expected student outcomes should include such skills as competence in self-directed learning, and mastery of oral communications, interpersonal relations, and intercultural maturity. "Data should be collected regularly to reveal pupil accomplishments, costs, professional accomplishments of teachers, utilization of facilities, and the like. Comparisons should be made with conventional schools of similar size, composition, and other similar characteristics" (Trump, 1969).

The rationale of the MSP (NASSP, 1969), had explicit sections on the evaluation of pupil progress and the evaluation of the whole school. The MSP standards for evaluation of pupil progress (appraisal, recording, and reporting) required that:

- Periodically, the school reports to parents, etc. the progress of each pupil in completing the *required* segments in the learning sequences of all the subject areas;
- Comparative test scores, standardized or local, are reported to show how the pupil has achieved in relation to others as based on various norms;
- What each pupil achieves beyond the required sequences is appraised and recorded; e.g., played on a team, completed a special study or project in given subject fields, participated in a play, or any other project not required of everyone.

The project asked its schools, in addition to or in place of letter grades, to report what each student actually knew or could do in basic areas of learning. It also urged teachers to evaluate special projects using such "affective goals" as creativity, persistence, use of resources, and value to others, rating where a student's placement fell on a continuum from the best the teacher had ever observed to the worst (Trump & Georgiades, 1970).

Project schools were also required to evaluate changes in the total program (school, community, home), in these areas:

- Changes in pupil learning roles, attitudes, interests, behaviors, etc.;
- Changes in teaching and supervisory roles, productivity, conditions, accomplishments, attitudes, etc.;
- Changes in community (including parents') perceptions of schooling, their attitudes, support, interest, etc.;
- Changes in utilization of learning and teaching resources in the school, community, and home, and utilization of money, time, spaces, etc., that affect learning, teaching, and supervision. (NASSP, 1969)

The project staff asked schools for regular reports about the implementation effects on students, staff, and program. It wanted to develop better methods and materials to evaluate changed conditions for learning, teaching, and supervision and to chronicle the effects of the program on students, teachers, and principals. Basically, the MSP proposed that schools evaluate each student's work in relation to his/her past achievement, and collect major formative data on the total program.

Most of the data that the MSP collected project wide were formative or process oriented in nature. Summative or product-oriented data were collected by the schools. Several sites developed comprehensive evaluation plans that included both formative and summative assessments as well as action plans for each year of the five-year project. Two of the MSP summary publications include detailed information about project-level and school-level evaluation efforts. Principals were invited to write articles describing what happened in their schools. Sixteen of the 34 participating schools submitted reports that were published as the November 1977 issue of the *NASSP Bulletin* (Volume 61, Number 412). The MSP also released a monograph entitled *How Good Is Your School?* by the project's associate director, William D. Georgiades (1978), with major assistance from James Keefe and other project participants. These publications offer the following information about MSP evaluation practices.

PROJECT-WIDE EVALUATION STUDIES

The evaluation design employed in the Model Schools Project had six elements:

- Assessing the understanding and commitment of participants to the project's design;
- Analyzing criterion-referenced data in relation to program objectives;
- Evaluating the adoption and following of a curriculum model;
- Measuring the use of a diagnostic-prescriptive-implementation-evaluative (DPIE) cycle;
- Collecting norm-based data; and
- Using competent outside visitors to the schools to observe certain identified areas and make reports on them (Georgiades, 1978).

Since our primary purpose here is to outline important concepts advocated by the MSP and to trace their relationships to present practices, we will not report the specific results of MSP evaluation efforts. Instead we will sketch some of the techniques that were used to implement them. The project staff authorized two doctoral dissertations at the University of Southern California to assess the levels of understanding of staff, students, and community in MSP schools. The most extensive formative study project-wide was completed in 1972 by B. Flavian Udinsky, James W. Keefe, and Jack L. Housden with data collected from 29 MSP schools. The study was replicated in 20 schools by George P. O'Brien (1974). Participants were asked to evaluate the implementation of seven areas of teacher role change (e.g., teacher-adviser, differentiated staffing), their attitudes toward the project, and factors contributing to or inhibiting full implementation of the desired role change. Project schools generally exhibited growth in understanding from the 1972 to the 1974 studies.

Criterion-referenced evaluation provides information about achievement of a standard or objective (like that in a driver's licensing examination). Individual rank in terms of others is not important here; meeting the criteria of the assessment is. The MSP developed a variety of instruments to evaluate the effectiveness of instructional assistants, large and small group activities, and instructional materials (especially learning packages/guides and learning contracts). Objectives and criterion measures were formulated for the seven major areas of the project (program strategies, structures, staffing, advisement, etc.). Diagnostic, criterion-referenced tests were used to place students properly in the subject matter sequences of the project's nine areas of learning. Some schools also prepared diagnostic tests for major content subdivisions to determine how students were doing in such subareas as writing, typing, or athletic skills, English literature, or contemporary United States history. Several schools validated the tests both for reliability and for longitudinal use during subsequent years of the project (content validity).

Time-log studies were conducted in 1974 and 1975 to ascertain how schools reorganized or restructured their schedules to establish a cycle of diagnosis, prescription, implementation, and evaluation. These time-activities-characteristics-products studies recorded the frequency of such student daily activities as talking informally, working, listening to teachers, participating in a discussion, using equipment, writing, reading, thinking, etc. Teaching behaviors were also logged to determine the degree to which teachers were functioning differently under the model. These studies validated the special importance of the teacher-adviser role—the close daily mentoring relationship between a teacher and some 20 to 30 students—and the crucial position of the school's supervisory-management team in providing instructional leadership and differentiated administrative supervision of the school's planned changes. "Use of time by students, teachers and the school management team shifted substantially during the five-year interval of the MSP. Realistically, the DPIE cycle would not have become a reality without such a shift" (Georgiades, 1978).

Finally, the MSP staff used university professors and trained graduate students as external auditors during the early years of the project to confirm the degree of progress or lack of it in the schools. Auditors were instructed to keep a low profile and to treat their findings with confidentiality. Gradually, schools were encouraged to assume more responsibility for their own evaluation. At the close of the project's fourth year, schools were asked to assess their own growth, particularly in the utilization of the teacher-adviser role and IS, and the degree of student involvement in the learning process. The result was growth in the ability of the schools to respond effectively to the needs of their students.

SCHOOL-SITE PROGRAM EVALUATION EFFORTS

Several MSP schools undertook major on-site evaluation efforts (NASSP, 1977).

- Bishop Carroll High School in Calgary, Alberta, Canada participated in two major evaluations by outside sources, one in 1972–1973 by a team from University of Southern California under the direction of Dr. Newton Metfessel, to set goals and objectives, to establish a formal evaluation plan for the school, and to evaluate selected cognitive and affective objectives. The study was repeated in 1973–1974. The second study, a total school evaluation conducted by the Alberta Department of Education in 1974, showed that Bishop Carroll had experienced considerable success in maintaining competitive levels of student achievement, in "humanizing education," and in developing reasonably high levels of student commitment to learning. Bishop Carroll continued to collect data throughout the project on various elements of its program.
- Edgewood Junior High School in Mounds View, Minnesota, followed a systematic evaluation plan for each year of the project that included a review and summary of all major decisions made during the year, student data and attitude surveys, S. R. A. student achievement tests, individual department evaluations, and a parent survey. The principal purpose of this data collection was to validate basic student achievement and to improve the program.
- Pius X High School in Downey, California, also had a comprehensive evaluation plan. Data were collected each year on all elements of the program beginning with a baseline year of 1970. Instrumentation included the SCAT-STEP tests of student aptitude and achievement, the Self-Concept as a Learner Scale measuring student motivation, study habits, and group orientation, student occupational aptitude and interest inventories, and yearly surveys administered to students, parents, teachers, and aides on the form-

ative (process) aspects of the project. In addition, each department developed and administered Curriculum Objective Referenced Evaluation (CORE) tests to assess the degree to which individual students had completed the "essential learnings" sequence according to school-established criterion levels.

- Wilde Lake High School in Columbia, Maryland, administered the Test of Academic Progress pursuant to the state's accountability law, with student mean performance ranging from the 70th to the 85th percentile in all subject areas. It also participated in numerous research studies as a model for the school district. Each year the University of Maryland compared Wilde Lake students with samples from other district schools. In addition, Johns Hopkins University conducted a two-year study designed to compare open organizations with less open ones. Wilde Lake students fared very favorably in all these studies.

All project schools made serious attempts to collect supportive data but some were less successful than those cited above because they lacked a systematic evaluation plan or experienced opposition to the program within the school or community.

EVALUATING STUDENT PROGRESS

In *A School for Everyone*, J. Lloyd Trump (1977) reemphasized what had been stressed many times to all schools of the MSP: that the true aim of all student assessment and progress reporting is "to help each student improve, regardless of potential and aptitudes." Trump saw traditional appraisal and grading as, at best, inadequate and, at worst, a comedy of errors. The traditional system measures competition among students rather than individual student progress. It facilitates computing student grade point average and rank-in-class but not student growth-in-knowledge. It encourages memorization of facts rather than the application of knowledge, creativity, and affective goals. It ignores *unique* student achievements like special projects and IS/research. And most damaging of all, it is simplistic and encourages superficial appraisal and simple-minded judgments of student achievement by parents, colleges, and employers.

The MSP proposed that schools gear their student appraisal and progress reporting practices to collecting the kind of data that would help students, their teachers, and their parents diagnose students' current knowledge and skills as the basis for improving them. The student was to be an active participant, not just an observer of the process. Specifically, Trump (1977) recommended a system that would be able to tell:

- Where the student is at a given time in the continuum of learning
- How the individual compares with other students
- What the student has done that was *not* required (Trump, 1977, p. 166)

The first element includes the quantity and quality of the work a student has been able to complete in all areas of the curriculum during a given period of time. The second element shows a student's performance on a variety of norm-based assessments such as reading examinations, typing, physical fitness, and fine arts skill tests. The third element reports on student special projects in all subject areas. No failures are reported because every student is on a continuum of continual progress, some faster, others more slowly. In the period of transition to the new system, options allowed for students, parents, colleges, and employers to request comparative grades, rank-in-class, and diploma certification.

Individual schools developed variations on these main elements. Wilde Lake High School in Columbia, Maryland, and Pius X High School in Downey, California, for example, marked students' work with A, B, and C, but no Ds and Fs. When a student failed to complete work, Wilde Lake recorded an incomplete or left the record blank; Pius X issued an IP (in progress). The Wilde Lake report card listed all courses and sequences in which the student was working, along with recorded grades, credit by sequences, the evaluating teacher or team, and other related information. The Pius X progress report listed total credit by sequence with the appropriate grades, as well as anecdotal information about student study habits furnished by subject-area teachers. Pius X parents received their students' progress reports at parent-faculty get-togethers three times each year. These meetings also provided opportunity for parent-student-teacher adviser conferences, either at this or at a later time (NASSP, 1977).

Mariner High School in Mukilteo, Washington, adopted a somewhat different system. Mariner eliminated the conventional A-B-C-D-F report entirely; no grades were given, but "honors" were bestowed on the high achieving. Each subject area was organized into 20 levels using "critical path" planning as pioneered by industry and the military. Students progressed through this curriculum continuum at their own pace and with opportunities for enrichment. A "mini-term" in the last six weeks of the school year offered many enrichment electives and encouraged students to complete their required work in the normal amount of time. Those who needed more time used the mini-term to complete their required levels (NASSP, 1977).

THE BIG SPLIT

The national educational climate of the late 1970s was focused on behavioral objectives, accountability, back-to-basics, and CBE. The latter was a movement to give specific meaning to the high school diploma in terms of explicit life-role learning outcomes. Although well intentioned, it turned out to be reductionist in the long run, pressuring communities to reduce their academic requirements to "minimal competencies." The tenets of the MSP tended to backfire in this environment. Many of the nuances were lost. In particular, the MSP evaluation concepts seemed lukewarm to many policy makers, too touchy-feely, not competency-based. In fact, MSP evaluation principles were highly performance-oriented and intended to support personalizing the learning environment.

Indeed, it is quite clear at this point that two distinct camps emerged that defined the pursuit of educational excellence in very different ways: (a) the "reductionists" who equated school quality with standardization, traditional practices, and evaluation based on norm-referenced tests; and (b) the "gestaltists" who advocate comprehensive renewal, personalized approaches to instruction, and evaluation based on performance or product. The former included (and still include) many conservative educators and projects, most policy makers and much of the public. The latter received its major impetus from the MSP, and is evident during the past 25 years in the work of the LECI, the IDEA, the University of Wisconsin CORS, the CES, and many other worthy efforts too numerous to mention in this limited treatment.

LEARNING ENVIRONMENTS CONSORTIUM INTERNATIONAL

The LECI, a MSP follow-up effort in the western parts of the United States and Canada, continues to advocate and update project concepts. Recall that many educational projects and programs falter because they fail to document student achievement. The MSP made no attempt to collect student achievement data project-wide. Many of the participating schools did collect and report on student achievement at the local level, but the public did not receive any aggregate data about the project as a whole. LECI attempted to fill this gap by adopting a comprehensive evaluation model to complement the other concepts advocated by the MSP.

LECI believes that an effective school must document:

- a well-defined philosophy,
- precise goals and objectives,
- a comprehensive school design,
- a defensible curriculum model,
- a systematic evaluation design, and
- clear-cut communication channels with students, staff, and public.

The LECI evaluation design incorporates both affective and cognitive measures, both formative and summative data. LECI schools have continued MSP criterion-referenced assessments, external audits, student growth-in-knowledge progress reporting practices, and local summative evaluation efforts. The summative measures in many LECI schools include several of what the U. S. Department of Education calls "measures of success": achievement test results, motivational and attitudinal scores, attendance, discipline and vandalism data, course enrollment and success rates, graduate follow-up studies, and program cost-effectiveness information. In addition, LECI adopted the CIPP Evaluation Model (*context-input-process-product*) for its internal and external evaluations (Stuffelbeam et al., 1971). This model directs that all planning decisions be supported by context evaluation (needs/problems assessment); all restructuring decisions, by input evaluation (resource use); all implementation decisions, by process evaluation (is the design in place and operating); and all redesign decisions, by product evaluation (actual accomplishments and achievements).

In its early years, LEC commissioned four project-wide evaluative studies to examine individual student growth as well as other variables in the school environment like climate and instructional strategies that might operate to raise or lower student achievement. The Scott Study (1975) compared the cognitive achievement of LECI students with that of students in more conventional programs using the SCAT-STEP tests of aptitude and achievement. No significant differences were found between the two groups, suggesting that students in LECI schools were achieving at levels comparable to more conventional programs. The other three studies looked at student attitudes toward internal/external "locus of control" of their lives as a result of exposure to varying amounts of IS, perceptions of school climate associated with staff personal characteristics and frequency of communication patterns, and the effect on school climate (particularly the students) of teacher-centered versus student-centered teacher behaviors. These studies enabled LECI schools to fine-tune their programs while keeping their public informed about student performance.

CENTER ON ORGANIZATION AND RESTRUCTURING OF SCHOOLS

Reductionists of the 1970s and 1980s argued that the educational reform movements of the past two decades may have been responsible for falling academic standards, reading levels, and SAT scores. Back-to-basics pressure reappeared and parallel movements such as CBE, MBO, and performance contracting sought to emphasize minimal competencies, standardized testing or external accountability. At the same time, others continued to maintain the momentum of comprehensive renewal.

The IDEA sponsored the League of Cooperating Schools in California under the leadership of John Goodlad as a clearinghouse of innovative practices and ideas, including many in evaluation and progress reporting. IDEA also sponsored the development of IGE at the University of Wisconsin (Madison) Research and Development Center (later the WCER). Like the MSP and LECI, IGE advocated a diagnostic-prescriptive approach to instruction and evaluation, with teachers as facilitators and advisers.

An agency of the Wisconsin Center, in the 1990s, took the next big step toward the kind of valid and equitable evaluation advocated earlier by the MSP. The CORS conceptualized what has been called "authentic" assessment, instruction, and student performance. We will concentrate here on what the Center discovered about standards of student performance and how to assess it. The Center defined *authentic academic achievement* in terms of three criteria of intellectual quality: (a) how learners construct knowledge, (b) the depth of the knowledge base or discipline, and (c) the meaning of the achievement apart from school. It further determined the *authenticity* of mathematics and social studies written assessment tasks based on seven general standards derived from these criteria (Newmann et al., 1995):

Construction of Knowledge
    1. Organization of Information
    2. Consideration of Alternatives
Disciplined Inquiry
    3. Disciplinary Content
    4. Disciplinary Process
    5. Elaborated Written Communication
Value Beyond School
    6. Problem Connected to the World
    7. Audience Beyond the School.

Assessment under this model consists in the actual performance of students on assigned or selected tasks. An example from Newmann and colleagues (1995, pp. 40–41) that scored high on several of these standards will give the reader a concrete idea of this evolution in evaluation.

Mathematics Example

In a fourth-grade mathematics class, students were assigned to figure the costs of running a household on no more that $2,000 per month. The teacher gave students a list of typical categories for expenses including rent, groceries, electricity, and phone. They were to determine actual costs by looking through a real estate guide for rent, choosing groceries from a local store's price list, etc. Students constructed budgets by examining the materials and discussing the possibilities with one another. . . . Students had to look at real costs and make priority choices in creating their budgets. . . . The activities connected mathematical content to decisions that students would need to make in life beyond school.

The content of the instruction is the basis for the evaluation. Teachers assess the degree to which students understand and realize the intent of the activity. To complete the task successfully, the student must master it. No ranking is necessary nor any grade needed. Success is the criterion. The CORS Center encourages teachers to use these standards as guides in the design of their instruction and evaluation. The hope is that schools will better focus on authentic intellectual performance and learn to help students demonstrate authentic achievement.

THE COALITION OF ESSENTIAL SCHOOLS

The CES is another strong proponent of authentic assessment. The Coalition was founded by Theodore Sizer at Brown University in 1984. The CES was based on a set of nine common principles, one of which urges performance-based student assessment:

Teaching and learning should be documented and assessed with tools based on student performance of real tasks. The final diploma should be awarded upon a successful demonstration of mastery for graduation—an "Exhibition." As the diploma is awarded when earned, the school's program proceeds with no strict age grading and with no system of "credits earned" by "time spent" in class. (Sizer, 1996, pp. 157–159)

CES schools require that their students "exhibit" their work and *earn* their diplomas by public "exhibitions" of that work. Exhibitions are products or performances of student's actual work—accomplishments rather than representations, cultivated proficiencies and skills rather than test results, public demonstrations rather than lists of credits. The Model Schools Project anticipated this form of assessment in its call for appraising and recording what students achieved in the project beyond the required sequences. Of course, contemporary exhibitions go considerably beyond the special projects of the MSP to encompass the knowledge and skills of all the academic disciplines. In fact, the exhibition, and related performance assessments such as portfolios (selected compilations of student work), constitute the whole of student performance appraisal in this model, rendering traditional grading and progress reporting obsolete.

In a CES national website article, Kathy Simon (1999) presents a scene of a high school science room in a "high implementing" CES school. Some of the students in the room are running chemical analyses of local river water to test a working hypothesis that pesticide runoff has polluted the water and reduced its frog population. Other students are surfing the web for pertinent studies on the problem. The teacher moves from group to group, advising students to probe deeply and to reach beyond obvious conclusions. A local water management board has invited the students to present their findings and recommendations. They are determined to provide some real answers. Simon tells us that

> The science teacher does not have to worry that the time devoted to the project will prevent him from "covering" a number of other projects. Rather than assessing his students through tests that require memorization of a wide and disparate range of facts, this school assesses students based on public exhibitions, where depth of understanding is what gains high marks.

Francis W. Parker Charter Essential School in Devens, Massachusetts (co-founded by Theodore Sizer and his wife) has established rigorous performance standards based on state and national frameworks in eleven academic disciplines. Student work at Parker is assessed by portfolios using schoolwide standards and performance rubrics. Students advance through the six-year program at their own pace, achieving promotion through "Gateway Exhibitions." Seniors must also complete a Senior Project on a topic that they explore independently with the help of an outside mentor and present it to an audience as part of their Graduation Exhibition.

> In Year-end Assessments, teachers evaluate student progress in narrative form, and assess their work (as "Just Beginning," "Approaches," or "Meets") relative to the curricular standards for their Division. The school's comprehensive summary of these evaluations accompanies the Parker transcript, as does a cover letter in which students reflect on their own academic history. (Francis W. Parker School Website, 2001)

The transcript also notes the student's rate of progress and effort.

CES schools recognize that many other ways exist besides tests to assess student learning. Students of CPE in New York City, for example, must complete an exhibition at the end of each unit of work that reflects the school's essential question for the topic under study. The exhibition may consist of an oral presentation, a publication, a videotape, a performance, or any other medium of choice, but it must address the curriculum's objectives and be directed to a real audience. CPE students receive a list of potential exhibitions at the start of each trimester (Woods, 1992).

STANDARDS VERSUS STANDARDIZATION

A dichotomy still exists between those who support standardized testing as the primary basis for evaluating school quality and those who argue that a school must first personalize its program and then evaluate real student performance with authentic assessments. In January 2002, the United States Congress passed the No Child Left Behind (NCLB) Act, the latest version of the Elementary and Secondary Education Act (U.S. Department of Education Website, 2002). The new law provides for increased accountability based on standards-based testing, more choices for parents and students attending failing schools, and stronger emphasis on reading to ensure that every child can read by the end of the third grade. The Act is well meaning and many states have implemented the testing requirement, but in fact very little has changed in schools. To those who remember the competency-based movement of the 1970s, the progression is very familiar. Many of the competency tests of that earlier period were revised, and revised again, and then discarded, because students failed them in large numbers and schools failed to provide the instructional supports that would enable students to pass. Indeed, in some communities, school boards administered the tests to themselves, and they failed, in larger numbers than the students. Again, even with the NCLB, it is business as usual in the schools, but with more teaching to the tests and little time for education.

Other countries have tried broad-scale educational reform with considerable success, but founded on very different premises. Denmark, for example, began its initiative 10 years ago, not with new testing, but with a national conversation about values. Wagner (2003) reports that the Danish Ministry of Education promoted discussions throughout the country about what it meant to be an educated citizen in Denmark approaching the twenty-first century. Participants decided upon the skills that all students needed for a "knowledge economy" as well as to be contributing citizens in the Danish democracy. The Ministry encouraged the formation of many different kinds of secondary schools and colleges, all considered "college ready," that allowed students to achieve mastery in different ways. The Danes also created a national system of oral and written examinations—at both elementary and secondary levels—developed, administered, and scored by educators, usually from nearby schools or districts. The system does not use standardized tests and there are very few dropouts.

Granted, Denmark is a small country, but the parallels with the responsibilities delegated by NCLB to American states are hard to ignore. The starting point, however, was and should be a dialogue on values and standards, not standardized tests. Robert Marzano (Scherer, 2001) believes that

> Standards hold the greatest hope for significantly improving student achievement. . . . But we must make the distinction between identifying the knowledge and skills that a student needs to know to be considered knowledgeable in a certain subject area and mandating the level of knowledge and skills that all students must achieve. These are two separate issues. . . . We need a monitoring system that allows us to track student progress on specific standards. State tests aren't effective feedback

mechanisms. . . . Grades—whether letter grades or percentages or a combination of both—don't tell us much unless we know the criteria on which they are based. . . . In standards-based grading, you might still have, but not necessarily need, an overall score or letter grade. What you would have are rubric scores or percentage scores on specific standards that were covered in the course.

The current state of the art in evaluation and grading should be standards-based but not necessarily standardized. Sizer (1992) argues that

> To assume that national examinations provide the only way to improve the system is both arrogantly to overrate our ability to create decent mass tests and—when we make international comparisons—to engage in a tricky non sequitur, to argue that because nations we think produce better school graduates have national examinations, it is therefore the central presence of those examinations which primarily creates the quality we admire. . . . Exhibitions are, of course, themselves tests. Teaching to the test is eminently sensible if the test is worthy, and a travesty if the test is corrupt or mindless. The issue is how far the test can be from the student, from his or her family and community, from the professional teachers who know their students well.

We need standards adapted to the needs of local populations. Exhibitions, portfolios, and other forms of authentic assessment can be designed with a specific, local population of students in mind and validated in terms of a broad (state) standard. Since exhibitions are standards based and public, they can provide a responsible accountability, the kind of trustworthy explanation of local student achievement for which most parents and policy makers are searching.

MODEL SCHOOLS PROJECT REDUX

The MSP asked schools to collect data for assessment and reporting that would *help students, teachers, and parents diagnose student knowledge and skills in order to improve them.* The project wanted students to be active participants in the process. It urged schools to adopt assessments that would demonstrate where students were in their continuum of learning, how they compared with other students, and what they had accomplished that was not required. The project was interested in furthering student growth, not rank in class. It mandated no particular progress reporting scheme as long as what was adopted actually demonstrated individual student performance and growth in knowledge and skills. It espoused evaluation at the project and school-program level that measured changes in learning and teaching, in community perceptions of schooling, and in the utilization of the objects and resources of schooling.

We could trace the philosophical origins of much of contemporary authentic assessment to the MSP. Whether it be student self-evaluation, or a Descriptive Review of a Child, whether simple performance assessments like science experiments or presenting a skit, whether local graduation exhibitions or facilitated discussion techniques like the Collaborative Assessment Conference or the Tuning Protocol, whether school-designed portfolio assessment or project-developed procedures like the International High School Portfolio or the Digital Portfolio, the MSP would recognize and embrace them all.[1] Moreover, the MSP would fathom the motivation of policy makers who espouse standards-based testing but would balk at the high-stakes nature of much of it. Remember that the MSP recommended criterion/curriculum-referenced testing as one measure of student performance. Standards-based assessment is only a small step from CRT technology.

No one test can account for the many outcomes of schooling nor fulfill the needs of education's many constituencies. Schools want tests that provide real feedback on student growth and the quality of the school program; policy makers want tests that provide accountability, that sort out the good schools/systems from the bad. These aims— accountability for student learning and accountability for the system— are hard to reconcile. In any conflict like this, schools must rush to the defense of students and their learning.

Elliot Eisner (2003) muses that

> The function of schools is surely not primarily to enable students to do well on tests—or even to do well in school itself. . . . The really important dependent variables in education are not test scores or even skills

performed in the context of schools; they are the tasks students are able to complete successfully in the lives they lead outside of schools. . . . In fact, I would argue that the major aim of schooling is to enable students to become the architects of their own education so that they can invent themselves during the course of their lives.

J. Lloyd Trump would support that kind of reasoning.

NOTE

1. For more information on these authentic assessment practices, see *Personalized Instruction: Changing Classroom Practice,* by James W. Keefe and John M. Jenkins (2000), and *Authentic Assessment in Action: Studies of Schools and Students at Work,* by Linda Darling-Hammond, Jacqueline Ancess, and Beverly Falk (1995).

CHAPTER 10

School Structure

James W. Keefe

The MSP was very concerned about the "things of education"—money, time, numbers, spaces, materials. One of the earliest articles on the project by J. Lloyd Trump (1969) devoted three pages to a discussion of finances, school buildings, allocation of space in new and existing facilities, and some features of the building. Trump advised that

> The 'things' of education are extremely important. The quality of pupil learning, the professionalization of teaching, and the refinement of curriculum depend to a remarkable degree on how the presently available school monies are spent. . . . Financial input should be analyzed in terms of product output. . . . Improvement of learning comes when money is spent differently. So does the professionalization of teaching. . . . Money must be spent in accordance with carefully considered programs that are different, not for the sake of being different, but because of the care that has been devoted to their conception, operation, and evaluation.

Trump (1969) considered school facilities in some detail in this article. He mentioned several uneconomical features of conventional school buildings such as long corridors and large lobbies, cafeterias, and specialized study areas. To reduce costs, Trump recommended flexible scheduling arrangements and modified facilities to allow teachers and students to use the buildings more efficiently. Saving money on school buildings and grounds would free up funds for the more important educational equipment and supplies. Schools could be much smaller if more activities were scheduled in such community settings as libraries and other appropriate venues. The school would be an "evolving facility."

THE MODEL SCHOOLS PROJECT

Driven by a philosophy of "doing better with what you have," the MSP outlined changes in the people, program, and structure of its "schools of tomorrow." Trump (1977) argued that "the *program* and *people* of education should always take precedence over *structure*. Conventional schools tend to reverse that order." MSP schools were to spend neither more nor less than conventional schools. Project schools had no normative class size nor teacher–pupil ratio, no uniform room size, no conventional standards for numbers of library books, types of supplies and equipment, etc. Room size, layout, and equipment, for example, were to reflect their proposed use rather than some artificial architectural norm. And ideally these decisions were to be made at the school staff level with advice from the school SMT, not at the district level.

The MSP stressed that school structure utilization was crucial to the success of teaching and learning in a school and was a contributor to school excellence. School structure—time, numbers, spaces, money, and materials—was to serve people and program.

Time

Individualized for students; professionalized for teachers. Time use derives from the philosophy and vision of a school and affects the culture and the climate of the institution and its people. Numerous studies have determined that teachers talk about two-thirds of the time a traditional class is in session.

> A student who passively listens to teachers talk and to other students' answers, especially wrong answers, does not use time productively. A school system that schedules standard length class periods and controls the time by sounding bells every 30 or 60 minutes does not help students learn how to use time productively. (Trump, 1977)

The MSP proposed that schools could change the ways teachers and students spend their time by initiating more flexible forms of scheduling, reducing unproductive teacher talk, and increasing the amount of time students have for productive independent study, small group discussion, and work activities in the school, home, and community. The MSP recommended these strategies:

- Continuous progress learning arrangements based on self-pacing learning guides, year-round school availability, and systematic use of multiple learning environments in the school, community, and home;
- Individualized scheduling for students working with their teacher-advisers to plan their use of time rather than relying on centralized scheduling controlled by the district office; the school office schedules only large groups and small discussion groups;
- Pontoon Transitional Design schedules (Trump & Georgiades, 1970)—a "higher form of team teaching" that combined two or more subjects in a two to four period block of time; two or more teachers collaboratively organized the time using large group, small group, and independent study strategies; and
- Professionalization of teacher schedules and SMT activities, with decision making delegated to the appropriate level of action; decisions are made by teachers, department chairs, subschool or division coordinators, and principals/SMT members at their related levels of operation.

Numbers

Learning group size varies with the purpose of the activity.

The number of students that are assembled for a given task, remedial or special interest, varies with the needs and purposes of the students. The school design presents various teaching and learning activities with different numbers in groups, depending on purposes and needs rather than a predetermined size. A remedial group may have one or two persons or a dozen or more who need a particular kind of activity. A special interest group of a given size may meet for an extended period of time so that students can learn together, exchange ideas, display products, take field trips, or engage in a variety of other activities. (Trump, 1977)

Pedagogical purpose determined typical MSP group sizes:

- Large group presentations were scheduled for 40 to 100+ students for about 30 minutes each week in each of the eight or nine major areas of knowledge;
- Small groups of 15 to 20 students followed the large groups as soon as possible each week for about 30 minutes of "reaction discussion"; and
- Numbers of students in study and work centers varied widely according to the task, the purpose, or the locale; individuals might work alone, with one other, or even with three or four others; 10 or more might collaborate on a common topic or in remedial work.

Spaces

Size, type, and locale of learning spaces differ with purpose; some are open, some closed, but most are a combination, with movable walls, acoustical treatment, and lighting for ease of conversion. The MSP conception of the learning environment expanded to include the community and the home as well as conventional and modified spaces within the school (Trump & Georgiades, 1970). The project suggested a reallocation of school space to provide (for a school of 1260 students) two large group instruction spaces, 20 SGD spaces, as well as eight learning laboratories or resource centers for independent study, one for each of the "areas of human knowledge" of the MSP model. The MSP also envisioned resource centers for each important subdivision of the eight major areas, such as biology, chemistry, vocal and instrumental music, reading, etc., providing up to 25 such spaces in a school. Specialized spaces for close supervision, conferencing, and socializing would round out the new school. Ideally, building walls in new schools would be movable so various spaces could be created as needed.

- Most conventional classrooms became learning centers for IS (*study* centers for reading, listening, conversing, etc.; *work* centers where "tools of the trade" were available for science, gym, shop, etc.); some students were scheduled for supervised study and/or work in the community;

- Some regular classrooms were partitioned to provide three small group or conference rooms or several teacher offices and work-rooms;
- Corridors, lobby areas, and cafeterias were converted into IS areas when fire laws permitted; in some schools, the cafeterias and auditoriums became the LGP areas;
- Priorities for any new construction were based on what would produce the most effective teaching and learning for the largest number of students in terms of the MSP goals and objectives.

Money

Financial inputs were analyzed in terms of product-output with the goal of producing better outcomes from present expenditures. The MSP viewed the primary outputs as changes in the principal's role, teaching roles, individualized learning, and curriculum revision. Schools would measure the productivity of an expenditure by comparing the success of a particular program (such as the teacher as learning facilitator or adviser, or curriculum revisions) with findings on comparable but different programs in the *same* school in the past. Changes in productivity were to be measured from year to year. Most of these measures were process-oriented. The MSP generally left summative evaluation to the school.

The project rejected standard or norm-based spending formulas for school expenditures. It also argued that teachers deserved competitive salaries but that higher salaries in themselves did not assure higher school productivity. The MSP model specifically called for school finances and facilities to be used differently (Trump & Georgiades, 1970). School funds, equipment, and supplies should be better used. Allowing for start-up costs, schools should not necessarily spend more money but use existing funds more efficiently, thus insuring better accountability.

Materials

Purchase of supplies and equipment based on what best enhances teaching and learning in the school. Trump (1977) maintained that

Standard lists of equipment imposed by central business and purchasing offices are an educational curse as well as a waste of money. The

responsibility of these offices should be to hear salespersons and as-
semble information that teachers and administrators can use in determining which supplies and equipment are more useful and practical, as
well as financially feasible, for the needs of their school program.

Decisions about supplies and equipment were the province of teachers,
with help from the school's SMT. Teachers were to learn how to make
wise spending decisions from the ideas, sample materials, and evaluation instruments made available to them by central office staff. The MSP
urged that district budgetary procedures that required massive expenditures for the purchase of equipment and supplies at construction or on
an annual basis be changed to make funds available to teachers when
needed, as the program developed.

The MSP school design also emphasized "an enlightened and cooperative relationship with the community" (Trump, 1977). Student use
of equipment and supplies in the community (in offices, stores, factories, etc.) would supplement the materials available to the school from
customary tax sources. It was indeed a matter of "doing better with
what you had."

TRENDS IN SCHOOL STRUCTURAL ISSUES

The LECI carried on the MSP philosophy of structural utilization beginning in the mid-1970s. LECI advocated that building layout, space
usage, staffing patterns, and scheduling options be spelled out in detail.
Ultimately this led to the creation of a systems tool called a School Design Statement. The School Design Statement is a key element of a
comprehensive design-based process developed in the 1980s and 1990s
for the NASSP by James W. Keefe and Eugene R. Howard (1997). The
process is described in the NASSP book, *Redesigning Schools for the
New Century: A Systems Approach*. Schools employing the process
perform a literature search, collect comprehensive assessment data, and
prepare a written school design of 11 elements—three basic components that define the conceptual base for the design and eight systemic
components that detail the structure of the interdependent operations of
the school (Keefe & Howard, 1997).

The LEC has championed this process, which in many ways updates and enhances several core MSP design concepts. The School Design Statement requires explicit descriptors, among others, of a school's planned structure and organization, its leadership, management and budgeting processes, and its fiscal resources, physical plant, and equipment. The design process also calls for the assessment of school goals (mission and vision), school culture/climate, student goals and outcomes, and program cost-effectiveness. This data is made available to parents, community, and other school stakeholders along with more conventional measures of school accountability.

At the same time that LEC was assuming the MSP mantle, the field of educational administration was becoming more conscious of *outcomes* (what a school administration should produce) in addition to the more traditional elements of *process* (what a school administrator does) and *efficiency* (how an administrator does it). The school administrator was expected to be *effective*—to achieve the results envisioned by his or her board and clients (Landers & Myers, 1977). This concentration on outcomes led, in turn, to a growth in systems thought in school administration.

Systems concepts first appeared in the field of biology and were later applied to other sciences and to engineering, management, and the behavioral sciences (see Margaret Wheatley, *Leadership and the New Science*, 1992.) A system is a "set of interrelated elements" (Ackoff, 1971) or a "network of interdependent components that work together to accomplish the aim of the system" (Deming, 1993). A systems approach is a *way of thinking* that relates the "*whole* of a problem/task/operation/group and its interacting subparts, as well as analyzing, selecting, implementing, and monitoring the optimum alternative sequences/interactions/functions of component parts to achieve desired outcomes" (Landers & Myers, 1977).

The systems mode of thought was well suited to the systematic approach to school change advocated by the MSP. One would think that these two movements would have been logical allies, but in reality, a synergy was not achieved until much later with the development of the NASSP/LEC School Design Statement and NASSP's Comprehensive Assessment of School Environments Information Management System (CASE-IMS). In the short term, systems thinking led to such planning and problem-solving tools as Management Information Systems, Operations Research (OR), System Analysis, the Program Evaluation and Review Technique (PERT), the Critical Path Method (CPM), the Planning, Programming, Budgeting, and Evaluation System (PPBES), and MBO. Some of these tools were utilized in MSP schools and in many other schools and districts to analyze and manage the input-output variables of the organizations.

Much of the hoped-for impact of the MSP was blunted in the 1970s by the decidedly conservative policy environment. Many policy makers as well as the general public believed that the educational innovations of the late 1950s and the 1960s were to blame for a perceived drop in academic standards and failing school discipline, as well as falling SAT scores and reading levels, and a general absence in the student and adult population of the minimal skills needed to cope in modern society. A "back-to-basics" backlash developed with emphasis on the three "Rs" and movements such as CBE, MBO, and corporate-based school performance contracting. "Doing better with what you have" took a back seat to external forms of accountability and student standardized testing.

A more promising development in the same time period was influenced by current school renewal efforts, the desegregation movement, and a demand beginning in the 1960s for return of educational control to the local community. *School site management* is

> The idea that the local community of individual schools, in concert with the principal and professional staff, should make decisions regarding the use of personnel of the school, the use of funds for the instructional program, the type of instructional program, the evaluation of personnel, and, be active within the collective negotiations at the local school level."
> (Baldwin, 1993)

This approach flows directly out of the MSP concept that school structure should serve the people and the program of the school. Major city school districts from Miami–Dade County to Chicago to Los Angeles have worked to change the relationships of administrators and teachers with each other and with the community. Problems have arisen, of course, in redefining the legal rights of teachers (and their unions), the managerial prerogatives of building principals and leadership teams, and the specific roles of parents and the community in any shared leadership responsibilities. But on the whole, the movement toward school site management has exercised a positive influence—placing school structure once again at the service of the instructional program and the needs of special populations.

The effective schools research of the 1980s identified a "safe and orderly environment," including school facilities and student discipline, as "one of the key characteristics of an effective school" (Frase & Hetzel, 1990). This research "found a sense of quiet pride in high-achieving schools and a sense of caring that was reflected in the positive physical appearance of a school where repairs are made immediately" (Robinson, 1985, p. 18). This research emphasized safety and cleanliness more than flexibility in school structure but it demonstrated that an excellent instructional program and a safe and orderly environment tended to be linked. Even a superb academic program may be overshadowed, however, if a school's environment is unsafe or dirty. The effective schools research reinforced the importance of school structure to the overall success of a school's program.

In the 1990s, NASSP again raised its voice on the topic of school renewal with a special report in partnership with the Carnegie Foundation for the Advancement of Teaching, entitled *Breaking Ranks: Changing an American Institution* (NASSP, 1996). The report makes 82 recommendations for the improvement of American high schools under nine categories presented as purposes of high schools. The category, Organization and Time, deals specifically with the restructuring of space and time for a more flexible education. The report states that "the manner in which a high school organizes itself and the ways in which it uses time create a framework that affects almost everything about teaching and learning in the school" (NASSP, 1996). Virtually all of the following proposals look back directly to MSP recommendations on school structure:

1. High schools should create small units in which anonymity is banished.
2. Teachers should be responsible for no more than 90 students.
3. High schools should develop flexible scheduling.
4. The Carnegie unit should be redefined or replaced.
5. High schools should reorganize traditional departmental structure for a more integrated curriculum.

6. Each high school should develop alternatives to tracking and ability grouping without restricting its range of courses and learning experiences.
7. The academic program should extend beyond the high school campus.
8. Schools should operate on a 12-month basis.

No data are yet available on the extent of implementation of these and other *Breaking Ranks* recommendations, but the nature of the report and the prestige of its sponsors argue for a significant impact in the near future.

The turn of the twenty-first century has brought with it a growing involvement of state legislatures and the U.S. Department of Education in more and more aspects of educational control and accountability. As education moves into the new century, two widely differing philosophies and approaches to educational practice are vying for the heart and mind of schooling. One, ascribed to by many in public policy positions and dominant at present, argues that school structure and program should primarily support public accountability regardless of how that might impact student learning. The other, prevalent in many individual schools and widely accepted in Canada, holds that school structure and program must, above all, enhance student learning and the personalization of instruction. The two views are so diametrically opposed that little reconciliation appears to be possible at this time. If the past is any prologue, however, things will certainly change again.

WHERE WE ARE TODAY

The MSP view of "the things of education" has not survived intact during the past 30 years. Some of the MSP school structural elements still influence contemporary educational practice, but for the most part, they have not endured. These are the current trends:

Time

The vast majority of contemporary high schools employ a traditional or modified traditional schedule. In a 1992 survey of 3893 high schools (41% response rate), Gerald Kosanovic (1994) found that almost 96% of those responding had traditional schedules. Only 2.3% used some form of block scheduling (the majority in New Mexico, Utah, and Wyoming) and 1.7%, a modular type schedule with shorter periods (Kosanovic, 1994). Only a few American schools utilize an individualized or personalized schedule, most of them formerly associated with the MSP. Individualized timetables (schedules) are more common in Canada because of the impact of two MSP/LEC schools, Bishop Carroll High School of Calgary, Alberta and Thomas Haney Secondary Centre of Maple Ridge, British Columbia, and the influence of the Canadian Coalition for Self-Directed Learning (CCSDL). Many middle schools and some CES have adopted block schedules, but the MSP Pontoon Transitional Schedule has disappeared. Continuous progress learning arrangements exist only in LEC-related schools. Since most schools have relatively traditional student schedules, teacher schedules have also reverted to the conventional. Most schools lack SMT, but school-site management has tended to support the professionalization of relationships among administrators, teachers, and school community in some districts. Regional accrediting associations using the NSSE school improvement model call for the establishment of a leadership team to guide the self-appraisal process.

Numbers

Traditional scheduling has locked most of today's schools into self-contained classes, but class sizes are generally smaller than at the time of the MSP. The MSP triad of LG/SG/IS is gone, but LEC, CES, and many other schools still employ small group activities and IS/research as appropriate. A great number of middle and high schools use cooperative small groups in various subject areas. Most school libraries operate today as instructional materials centers, many with decentralized work centers for technology use and specialized career training. Forms of experiential and community-based learning still exist, along with school-sponsored student volunteer service.

Spaces

Most contemporary school buildings are still variations on traditional egg-crate architecture. Some districts/schools provide small group and seminar rooms and quiet spaces for IS and research. Schools built in recent years also have some magnificent specialized facilities including large theaters and technology labs. Districts are permitting more community-based experiences than in the past, provided these activities do not interfere with schools meeting their state testing targets. The MSP "school of the future" is largely a relic of the past, notwithstanding some excellent examples still thriving and multiplying in Canada.

Money

Product-output school budgeting is in vogue but not the MSP variety geared to changes in teacher and administrator roles and more productive approaches to curriculum and instruction. Rather, today's variety is geared to improving student scores on state standardized tests. In some school districts, curriculum and instructional planning have gone on almost permanent hiatus to enable teachers to teach to state tests. Standard spending formulas are back in style with poorer districts suffering the consequences. Teacher salaries are somewhat more competitive than 30 years ago but, not surprisingly, without any comparable rise in school productivity. Schools in more affluent communities have more and better buildings, equipment, and supplies. Those in less affluent areas continue to struggle. Jonathon Kozol (1991) writes poignantly of the glaring inequities between affluent and inner city school resources. Of the contemporary school renewal projects, the CES alone argues that school budgets should provide for substantial collective planning time for teachers (as well as competitive salaries) and for per-pupil costs no more than 10% greater than traditional schools. CES concedes that administrative plans may require the reduction or elimination of some services to accomplish this goal. LEC schools continue to support learning-responsive budgeting.

Materials

Purchasing in most districts remains very traditional and centralized. Most teachers do not have much control over the nature of their equipment and supplies, although the quality is usually high and appropriate in more affluent districts. School-site management districts offer administrators and teachers more flexibility in managing the "things of education" than their equivalents in more conventional districts. Some schools/districts have cultivated admirable relationships with their communities, resulting in regular student placement in local offices, stores, and factories for student service and career training.

The MSP urged schools to "do better with what you have." We must await a new wave of school renewal to see if this axiom acquires greater currency in the future than it has achieved in the recent past.

CHAPTER 11

Retrospective
Robert B. Amenta

If schools are to meet today's challenges, they must find ways to make learning more intellectually challenging while meeting the diverse needs of the students who bring with them varying learning styles and talents. Students entering our complex society must have problem-solving skills and the confidence that they can be successful. H. G. Wells stated that human history is a race between education and catastrophe. If we are to avoid catastrophe and win the race, then we must work to continuously improve our schools.

COMPREHENSIVE SCHOOL REFORM

The last half of the twentieth century witnessed many attempts to reform the nation's schools. These reforms followed a period of retrenchment in the wake of the backlash to John Dewey's Progressive Education movement. Many of Dewey's ideas concerning relevancy and student interaction with content reemerged in the 1960s and 1970s through the guidance of the NASSP. With his engaging personality and leadership skill, J. Lloyd Trump led the way as director of the NASSP MSP; it is rare when such an individual, with both vision and action, comes upon the scene. Many decades separate John Dewey's "Eight-Year Study" and J. Lloyd Trump's Model Schools Project, yet the methodologies they propound are connected. Trump and his associate director William D. Georgiades strongly advocated that school change must be comprehensive rather than incremental (Trump & Georgiades, 1978). A total Gestalt must take place in order to drive change in student achievement.

The directors cited research indicating that changing a single element in a school would not make a significant difference in student achievement. Change must occur simultaneously in the areas of principal role, student role, teacher role, curriculum, facilities, and evaluation. Only changing the total school environment would improve student growth. The participants in the MSP attempted to design a school model that would guide them in rethinking the roles of school constituents and the schools' organizational structure, and although the project has been widely emulated it has had limited continuous success; the task was much more formidable than Trump and Georgiades had anticipated.

The 36 schools selected to participate in the MSP agreed to implement the model and carefully assess their progress. The participating schools' trustees, the superintendents, the principals, teachers, and parents all supported the initiative; however implementation was difficult to achieve. Willingness, support, and effort were not enough to overcome the unique characteristics of the school environment. A school's unique characteristics can become barriers to comprehensive change, and therefore change agents must learn and use new methods that work with the school environment rather than trying to overcome it. Recent organizational studies have shown that organizations go through significant design deviations over time as they adapt to local conditions. The amount of deviation is dependent upon the number of individuals involved and the number of factors that need to be supported. Organizational research has shed light on why this phenomenon occurs. A rationalist linear approach to restructuring is often the victim of chaos and random circumstances that are not foreseen. As Phillip Schlechty (1990) has stated,

> I believe that the act of leadership is, in part, an effort to impose order on chaos, to provide direction to what otherwise appears to be adrift, and to give meaning and coherence to events that otherwise appear, and may in fact be, random.

Today, educators understand that one model will not fit all schools. Successful programs are not transferable as was once believed. It is even difficult to transport specific facets of programs. This is not to suggest that the MSP failed to contribute to school improvement; certainly, this book is a testament to all those who are working diligently in schools and making significant progress. Indeed, many of the ideas proposed by the model are evident in many of the current reform initiatives. The ideas can be found in many public and private schools across the United States and Canada. In fact, the core MSP elements are the foundation of many current comprehensive school reform projects. The ideas are transferable when they are adjusted to meet the unique designs of individual schools. One design does not fit all schools; rather, lasting change is the product of school stakeholders planning together to solve their own specific needs guided by past successes.

Modern school management theory suggests that schools should be viewed as living, evolving organisms, constantly reacting to their changing environment. So much of the environment is outside the control of the school that it is impossible to design a long-term fixed plan. The Trump model initially was such a fixed design; however, the leaders soon acknowledged that local adjustments were necessary. Even with this recognition, the schools were encouraged to stay close to the model. Real, and constant, school improvement involves the capacity to change in the face of arising circumstances. As described in previous chapters, the LEC, founded in 1974, continues the legacy of the NSSP MSP. It recognizes many of the valuable ideas proposed and attempted in the 1960s; however, it does not suggest a rigid model, because it recognizes that each school is different and must adapt to the constantly changing environment. The LEC Design/Redesign strategy acknowledges that schools are constantly changing and complex organizations. This consortium encourages reflective adaptation to shifting circumstances and emerging knowledge. LEC is committed to the process of total school design/redesign rather than a specific predetermined outcome. The design model guides the management team in developing a unique school learning organization.

Ted Sizer's CES (2000a), similar to MSP and LEC, joins in endorsing comprehensive reform as a necessity for school improvement. The model requires that participating schools adhere to 10 guiding principles. These principles serve as blueprints to help schools design an organization that meets the needs of their particular community within the specific local context.

CHANGING ROLES AND RESPONSIBILITIES

One of the key components of the MSP was the differentiated roles of the principal, teacher, student, and instructional assistant. There was a conscious effort to move away from teacher-directed instruction to student-engaged learning. This instructional change was based on the belief that the schools could not meet modern-day challenges until the people within them changed the way they think and act. Improving the school culture and redesigning the facilities would only provide an environment for change; the individuals at the school site must take advantage of the opportunity to do things in a different manner.

Principal's Role

The principal in the model school was expected to be the instructional leader who possessed the requisite skills, capacities, and vision to lead change, not follow it. The role shift was from one of management and administration to a focus on leadership and facilitation of the teaching and learning process. Today, school leadership has evolved from a focus on management to a focus on instruction. Specific skills required for principals are outlined in the standards of the Interstate School Leaders Licensure Consortium (ISLLC) in conjunction with the NASSP Twenty-first Century School Administrator Skills. In reality, the principal must be a manager, instructional leader, visionary, politician, strategist, community leader, and personal counselor.

In their literature review, Wanzare and Da Costa (2001) concluded that the majority of writers agreed that there are over 38 major roles performed by principals. Teachers, parents, students, and central office staff have varying expectations of the principal. This multiplicity of roles and expectations tend to fragment principals' actions and time allocations. Hallinger and Murphy (1987) concluded that the principal's job definition involves too many different work activities, causing fragmented interactions with the many different actors. The MSP, CES, LEC, and many other reform models emphasize instruction while promoting the sharing of the numerous tasks necessary to keep the school operating on a daily basis. Shared decision making and participatory management styles are necessary to create a problem-solving school environment. Without shared decision making, the tasks are too formidable for one individual to accomplish.

Teacher Role

The goal of all reform is to improve student learning, and central to this goal is the relationship between the teacher and the student. The role of the teacher as one who provides information and directs the class from the front of the room is no longer viable. Student learning will not improve until the relationship between the teacher and student changes. Central to the MSP model is the teacher as adviser to a small group of students. The teacher-adviser meets with the students on a regular basis and attempts to know them well. As Sizer (1999) explained,

> I cannot teach students well if I do not know them well. Each of my adolescent students is in the midst of a growth spurt and the struggle for independence that characterizes every person's route from childhood to adulthood. Each is a complex and evolving human being. Each learns in a somewhat different way.

The teacher/advisory role is perhaps the most successful element in Trump's plan. The idea that the teacher is an adviser and knows each child's ability is also widely replicated by today's reform models. The advisory role is an attempt to meet the needs of the diverse learners in our classrooms, and as Holm and Horn (2003) emphasized, the diversity of learners increases the importance of knowing who those students are and how they learn in a global society. Darling-Hammond, Fuhrman, and O'Day (2002) described the advisory role at Central Park East Secondary School as one of the school's key strategies for ensuring that the diversity of students cannot be overlooked. Each professional staff member at CPESS works over a period of two years with a group of 12 to 15 students and their families, providing academic and personal supports of many kinds. Accelerated Schools and the Consortium of Essential Schools also call for a close relationship between students and teachers with frequent, high-quality academic interactions among teachers and students.

The size of today's schools makes it difficult for counselors and administrators to know the students well. Student dropout rates, low attendance, and discipline problems result when students are anonymous and feel disconnected from the school. As Jenkins stated, it is the adviser-advisee relationship that provides the students with an advocate who knows the student well and can act in his/her best interests. Allowing the teacher-adviser and student to remain together throughout the student's school experience helps the bond grow over time. Frequent individual conferences with the student and parents aid communication. This sharing of information assists the advising process.

Student Role

The MSP proposed that students take responsibility for their learning under the direction of a teacher-adviser. The intentions of the model were to help students use their minds by motivating them through continuous progress arrangements and self-direction. This goal is common among many of today's reform models. The Paideia schools encourage discovery learning with the individual assistance of teachers and other adults. Trump viewed the student role as worker with adult guidance; he believed that students should not be passive receptacles but rather engaged active learners (Trump, 1969). The MSP included three major instructional components designed to engage students in their learning endeavors.

Lowery (1996) described the student's daily routine, with large group presentations, small group seminars, and independent study as the means by which the student engages in his or her own quest for knowledge. Mortimer Adler (1982) proposed a similar design, in his widely adopted Paideia Proposal. The large group presentation by teachers, students, and other adults was the "good didactic approach" described by David Perkins (1992) when observing Paideia schools. These presentations were designed to motivate students to seek and expand their knowledge. The small group seminars consisted of 10–15 students who met to discuss and share information and ideas that were generated from the large group presentations or from their independent study. Individual study provided students with the time to pursue their interests and learning while guided by the teacher.

School Schedule

Trump (1977) believed that the secondary school schedules place students and teachers in rigid structures that inhibited learning. He envisioned a flexible schedule that changed as the needs of the learners and teachers demanded. During the decades following Trump's writing, many public and private schools utilized flexible schedules in an effort to create opportunities that would allow large group, small group, and independent study. Trump suggested that the schedule should reflect the learning styles of the students, as well as the styles of the teachers and the content being studied. Trump recommended that schools use computers to organize the schedule into 15- or 20-minute modules of time, although he emphasized that the class periods need not be equal. He stated that the students should attend 18 to 20 hours of large and small group instruction with an additional 12 hours devoted to independent study. Dr. Trump's plan was to be viewed as a guide, and he warned that educators should be aware that even a flexible schedule could become a rigid format. Donald Hackmann stated in a previous chapter that "A scheduling model can empower teachers and students to experience learning in creative, motivating ways, or it can be restrictive and repressive, forcing teachers to formulate lessons that will fit into the confines of rigid, unyielding time increments."

Mortimer Adler (1982) describes the use of time in terms of instruction delivery. According to Adler's Paideia proposal, 10% to 15% of the time should be devoted to didactic instruction. This refers to factual information given to the students by means of lecture, videos, and assigned readings. Intellectual coaching is a key element of the proposal; 60% to 70% of the students' time is spent in coaching situations. Coaching is guidance through modeling and questioning. The goal is for students to acquire expertise in skills such as reading, writing, calculating, and observing by questioning, as well as learning via feedback. The third element of the proposal is the seminar, and it occurs approximately 15–20% of instructional time. The seminar is a collaborative, intellectual dialogue facilitated by open-ended questions about the content.

Curriculum Design

Trump stated that information on research-based practices would facilitate program choices. He recommended that the content be differentiated according to (a) basic (essential) for all student to know in all subject areas, (b) desirable (elective), and (c) enriching (career-oriented). Educators, for example, who are interested in a strong academic focus across curricular areas (basic) will find this the focus of Core Knowledge or the Paideia Proposal. These two programs, however, differ in the number and type of classroom practices they use. Paideia employs cooperative learning, didactic instruction, and teachers as learning facilitators. Core Knowledge is less directive concerning classroom practices. For educators interested in coordinating academic and related services, School Development or Community for Learning are possible choices (Wang, Haertel, & Walberg, 1998). Desirable elective and enriching experiences are evidenced in the CES program. LEC continues to advocate self-paced, continuous progress arrangements with plenty of opportunity for interactive, collaborative, and reflective learning experiences.

The polarized conflicting perspectives described by English and Keefe in chapter 6 can be witnessed in the schizophrenic behaviors of our public schools. Designing educational environments to enable students to discover and celebrate their differences seems the business of schools in the twenty-first century. Lifelong learning implies a devotion to actualizing one's unique talents, and school seems a likely place for getting a jump-start on this process.

The Federal and State governments are demanding allegiance to norm-referenced testing on prescribed knowledge while teachers find it impossible to ignore the personal needs of their students. A national dialogue is needed to build consensus and conceptualize the belief that the essentials (measured facts) are seen as minimal and only part of a student's continuous path toward individual growth. The current path toward standardization and minimalism leads away from individual differences, maximizing talents and celebrating American individualism.

Personalization

The efforts to improve schools over the last 50 years have been enormous. A great amount of time and money has been expended in the hope of raising standards and making the school a better place for students. The key issue in most attempts to restructure has been the underlying belief that education must be personalized. Small schools with reduced class size are believed to create an environment where learning will flourish. The reality is that schools have become larger and more impersonal, and reduced class size has been elusive. LEC has worked diligently trying to restructure the organization so that personalization can become a reality. Technology is now readily available to help meet the student's individual needs. It is difficult for the older generation to comprehend the personal relationship that today's cyber-students have with their computer. Students interact with the Internet emotionally and cerebrally. They go there to meet friends and acquire new ones. It is their instant resource for information and communication. Schools must tap into this phenomenon or lose out to its growing popularity. If the schools fail in their quest for personalization, the Internet will draw students from in-class to online, and they eventually will travel cyberspace never to return to the bricks and mortar.

School Culture and Climate

The NASSP's Task Force on School Climate, cited by Keefe and Howard (1997), defined "climate" as "the relatively enduring pattern of shared perceptions about the characteristics of an organization and its members." This is consistent with the MSP thrust to improve the "ethos" of schooling. LEC advocates that schools pursue a local, design-based planning process and develop a School Design Statement that includes specifications for school culture and climate. Anyone visiting a number of schools will immediately feel the "ethos" described by J. Lloyd Trump. Today one hears the word "climate" wherever educators gather. The present challenge is not only to acknowledge the unique culture existing in each organization; it is the quest to understand and then change the culture in a positive way. Education leaders can recognize many of Trump's ideas in their understanding of climate. Owens (2003) proposes that school climate is the overlapping and interaction of four dimensions or subsystems in the organization; these subsystems are ecology, structure, milieu, and culture, and when each is defined one can identify many of the elements in Trump's (1969) model—elements such as communication patterns, decision-making patterns, technology, leadership, values, norms, and pedagogical inventions.

Evaluation

J. Lloyd Trump (1969) understood the importance of research as a tool to bring about school change. His plan included two areas of evaluation that would guide the schools and provide valuable feedback.

The first evaluation proposed included appraisal, recording, and reporting of pupil progress. It called for periodic reports to parents and other school stakeholders regarding the progress of each pupil in completing the required segments in the learning sequences of all subject areas, including comparative test scores, standardized or local, to show how the pupil had achieved in relation to others as based on various norms, as well as assessment of student achievement beyond the required sequences.

The second evaluation involved the assessment of the total school program, including

- Changes in pupils' learning roles, attitudes, interests, behaviors
- Changes in teaching and supervisory roles, productivity, conditions, accomplishments, attitudes
- Changes in utilization of learning and teaching resources in the school, community, and home; utilization of money, time, spaces, etc. that affect learning, teaching, and supervision

In years to come schools will provide many more options based on diagnoses and prescriptions with evaluation patterns that lead to further improvements for both individuals and institutions. The monolithic structure of secondary schooling will diversify in the next decade. (Trump & Georgiades, 1978)

The above statement by Trump and Georgiades (1978) was made at the conclusion of their "Model Schools Project Report." Unfortunately, the monolithic structure of secondary schooling is moving in the opposite direction. Accountability, standards, and high-stakes testing have as much to do with politics, wealth, and power as they do with consensus building in the best interest of students. A study by Dana Rapp (2002) indicated that the views expressed by board-certified teachers confirm the extent to which an overwhelming number of extremely caring, committed, and creative educators have come to believe that education is headed in an unhealthy direction. They overwhelmingly agree that professionals and parents are losing an enormous amount of autonomy and voice.

Shared Management

Membership in the MSP required commitment from the school board, the superintendent, the community, and school personnel. Sustained commitment from these constituents was difficult to achieve. Group membership continues to evolve, with less commitment by the new members who perhaps do not understand or believe in all of the change components. Nevertheless, this commitment is required from all of the change models today. It is commonly believed that all of the school stakeholders must share the vision and the process of the reform being attempted. Without this common focus, the school is hampered by conflicting purposes. Stable district leadership must support comprehensive reform efforts. The RAND study of the New American Schools (NAS) (Berends, Bodilly, & Kirby, 2002) reform project found that there were large differences in implementation among schools due in part to the level of district support. "In general, implementation was higher in those districts that were more supportive of the NAS designs and that were characterized as having stable district leadership that backed the reform and made the reform central to its improvement efforts."

Comer School Development Program emphasizes the need for schools to plan through a team approach, with the "team" consisting of all stakeholders. Under the leadership of psychiatrist James Comer, the Child Study Center of Yale University sponsors the School Development Program, which provides coaching, networking, training, and other support services to schools that are seeking to improve their effectiveness. The School Development Program started in 1968 in the two lowest-achieving schools (which were virtually in Yale's backyard) in New Haven. By 1999 the program had grown to a network of 721 schools, mostly K–6 but also some middle schools and high schools; research and evaluation indicate that the program is effective in increasing academic achievement, improving behavior, increasing attendance, and bolstering the self-concept of students. The basis of the program is

- school planning and management team
- student and staff support team
- parent team promotes the involvement of parents in all areas of school life

The program emphasizes the development of an organizational culture in the school that is characterized by no-fault problem solving, consensus decision making, and collaborative working relationships.

CONCLUSION

It is difficult to draw conclusions about comprehensive school reform because of the complexities involved. As explained by Schwartzbeck (2002), "The complexities of measuring student achievement and other outcomes, the difficulties found when schools are moving targets, and the unique ways schools adopt reform present many obstacles to discerning trends." The past two decades have seen a call for getting tough with schools. The reformers call for longer school days, longer school years, more homework, fewer electives, high school exit exams, competency standards, higher college entrance requirements, and more school accountability.

Trump and Georgiades (1978) provided a retrospective of the MSP and recognized the reluctance of schools, and the people associated with them, to change. They urged all stakeholders to work together for school improvement and for all students.

We emphasize the necessity of increased cooperation of all persons in school systems. Teachers have basic roles in school improvement. Cooperation and open, active, and positive working relationships between them and the supervisory management team, which includes their department chairpersons, are essential. Central office persons set the tone of the school system. The emphasis needed is on diversity among schools to help each one to develop a program best suited to the area served. Students, their parents, and local groups need bona fide reasons to become involved positively in program improvements. The leadership team helps to make the whole operation productive of positive outcomes.

It is interesting to note that as reform models are proposed and discussed by educators and the general pubic, the ideas presented four decades ago are reemerging as viable and worthy of consideration. Yesterday's experiences are not always the answers to today's problems; however, as we all seek to better meet the needs of our students, we should be mindful of the lessons of the past. This book is an attempt to honor the past and envision the future. We don't know all the answers yet, but what we do know now is that schools need not start from scratch in designing effective schoolwide plans. A wide array of promising programs is available, backed up by national networks of trainers, fellow users, materials, assessments, and other resources.

Change is difficult, and trailblazers need to have the courage to take risks. Trailblazers such as J. Lloyd Trump, William Georgiades, and their NASSP colleagues, as well as the reformers who followed them, deserve our respectful support and continued encouragement.

References

Ackoff, R. L. (1971, July). Towards a system of systems concepts. *Management Science, 661.*

Adler, M. (1982). *The Paideia proposal: An educational manifesto.* New York: Macmillan.

Aiken, W. M. (1942). *The story of the Eight-Year Study.* New York: Harper and Brothers.

Airasian, P. W., & Walsh, M. E. (1997). Constructivist cautions. *Phi Delta Kappan, 78,* 444–449.

American Youth Policy Forum. (2000). *High schools of the millennium.* Washington, DC: Report of the American Youth Policy Forum.

Andrews, R., & Soder, R. (1987). Principal leadership and student achievement. *Educational Leadership, 44*(6).

Arygris, C. (1982). *Reasoning, learning, and action.* San Francisco: Jossey-Bass.

Baldwin, G. H. (1993). *School site management and school restructuring.* Topeka, KS: National Organization on Legal Problems of Education.

Bass, B. (1985). *Leadership and performance beyond expectations.* New York: Free Press.

Beck, L., & Murphy, J. (1993). *Understanding the principalship.* New York: Teachers College Press.

Bennis, W. (1989). *On becoming a leader.* Reading, MA: Addison-Wesley.

Bensman, D. (2000). *Central Park East and its graduates.* New York: Teachers College Press.

Berends, M., Bodilly, S., & Kirby, N. S. (2002, October). Looking back over a decade of whole-school reform: The experience of new American schools. *Phi Delta Kappan, 84*(2), 168–175.

Bishop Carroll High School (2002–2003). *Partial Outline of English 10 Course.* Unpublished manuscript. Calgary, Alberta.

Brill, J., Kim, B., & Galloway, C. (2001). Cognitive apprenticeships as an instructional model. In M. Orey (Ed.), *Emerging perspectives on learning, teaching, and technology.* Athens: University of Georgia. (http://studio.coe,uga.edu/book/CognitiveApprenticeship.htm.)

Brookover, W. B. (1982). *Creating effective schools. An in-service program for enhancing school learning climate and achievement.* Holmes Beach, FL: Learning.

Brooks, J. G., & Brooks, M. G. (1993). *In search of understanding: The case for constructivist classrooms.* Alexandria, VA: Association for Supervision and Curriculum Development.

Brown, A. D. (1995). *Organizational culture.* London: Pitman.

Brown, J. S., Collins, A., & Duguid, P. (1989). Situated cognition and the culture of learning. *Educational Researcher, 18*(1), 32–42.

Brubacher, J. S. (1947). *A history of the problems of education.* New York: McGraw-Hill.

Buckman, D. C., King, B. B., & Ryan, S. (1995). Block-scheduling, a means to improve school climate. *NASSP Bulletin, 79*(571), 9–18.

Burns, J. M. (1978). *Leadership.* New York: Harper & Row.

Canady, R. L., & Rettig, M. D. (1995). *Block scheduling: A catalyst for change in high schools.* Princeton, NJ: Eye on Education.

Carnegie Council on Adolescent Development's Task Force on Education of Young Adolescents. (1989). *Turning points: Preparing American youth for the 21st century.* Washington, DC: Carnegie Council on Adolescent Development.

Carroll, A. W. (1975). *Personalizing education in the classroom.* Denver, CO: Love.

Carroll, J. M. (1989). *The Copernican plan: Restructuring the American high school.* Andover, MA: The Regional Laboratory for Educational Improvement of the Northeast and Islands.

CES National Website. (2002a). *About the coalition of essential schools.* (www.essentialschools.org/lpt/ces_docs/22).

CES National Website. (2002b). *The common principles.* (www.essential schools.org/pub/ces_docs?about/phil/10cps/10cps.html).

Chawla, S., & Renesch, J. (Eds.). (1995). *Learning organizations: Developing cultures for tomorrow's workplace.* Portland, OR: Productivity.

Clerk, F. E. (1928). *A description and outline of the operation of the adviser–personnel plan at New Trier High School.* (limited distribution) Winnetka, IL.

Coleman, J. S. (1966). Equity in educational opportunity. *NASSP Bulletin, 536,* 111–119

Colia, C. B. (2001). *The relationship between culture, climate, and school effectiveness*. Unpublished doctoral dissertation, University of Colorado.

Council of Chief State School Officers. (1996). *Interstate School Leader Licensure Consortium: Standards for School Leaders*. Washington, DC: Author.

Creswell, J. (1997). *Creating Worlds: The Scottish Storyline Method*. Portsmouth, NH: Heinemann.

Cubberly, E. P. (1916). *Public administration*. Boston: Houghton Mifflin.

Cushman, K. (1990) Are advisory groups essential? What they do, how they work. *Horace*. Providence, RI: The Coalition of Essential Schools.

Dalin, P. (1973). *Changing the school culture*. London: Cassell.

Dantley, M. (1990). The ineffectiveness of Effective Schools leadership: An analysis of the Effective Schools movement from a critical perspective. *Journal of Negro Education*, *59*(4), 585–598.

Daresh, J. C. (2002). *What it means to be a principal: Your guide to leadership*. Thousand Oaks, CA: Corwin.

Darling-Hammond, L. (1993, June). Reframing the school agenda: Developing the school agenda: Developing capacity for school transformation. *Phi Delta Kappan*.

Darling-Hammond, L. (1997). *The right to learn: A blueprint for creating schools that work*. San Francisco: Jossey-Bass.

Darling-Hammond, L., Ancess, J., & Falk, B. (1995). *Authentic Assessment in action: Studies of schools and students at work*. New York: Teachers College Press.

Darling-Hammond, L., Fuhrman, S. H., & O'Day, J. A. (2002). *Reward and reform*. San Francisco: Jossey-Bass.

Deal, T. E. (1982). *Corporate cultures: The rites and rituals of corporate life*. Reading, MA: Addison-Wesley.

Deal, T. E. (1987). The culture of schools. In *Examining the Elusive*. Yearbook. Alexandria, VA: Association for Supervision and Curriculum Development (ASCD).

Deal, T. E. (1993). The culture of schools. In M. Sashkin & H. Wahlberg (Eds.), *Educational leadership and school culture*. Berkeley, CA: McCutchan.

Deming, W. E. (1993). *The new economics for industry, government, education*. Cambridge, MA: Massachusetts Institute of Technology.

Dykema, R. (2002, May, June). *How schools fail kids and how they could be better.* An interview with Ted Sizer. *Nexus* online journal (www.nexuspub.com/articles/2002/may2002/interview1.htm).

Edmonds, R. (1979, October). Effective schools for the urban poor. *Educational Leadership, 37*(1), 15–24.

Edmonds, R. (1986) Characteristics of effective schools. In U. Neiser (Ed.), *The school achievement of minority children*. Hillsdale, NJ: Erlbaum.

Education Commission of the States. (1998). *Comprehensive school reform: Identifying effective models.* Denver, CO: ECS.

Educational Research Service (2000). *The principal, keystone of a high-achieving school: Attracting and keeping the leaders we need.* Report prepared for the National Association of Elementary School Principals and National Association of Secondary School Principals.

Eisner, E. W. (2003). Questionable assumptions about schooling. *Phi Delta Kappan, 84*(9), 648–657.

Elmore, R. F. (1995). Teaching, learning, and school organization: Principles of practice and the regularities of schooling. *Educational Administration Quarterly, 31,* 355–374.

English, F. W. (1989). A school for 2088. In H. J. Walberg & J. J. Lane (Eds.), *Organizing for learning: Toward the 21st century.* Reston, VA: National Association of Secondary School Principals.

English, F. W. (1993). Changing the cosmology of the school schedule. In L. W. Anderson & H. J. Walberg (Eds.), *Timepiece: Extending and enhancing learning time* (pp. 23–34). Reston, VA: National Association of Secondary School Principals.

ERIC Clearinghouse on Educational Management. (1993, September). *Survey of major issues and trends relevant to the management of elementary and secondary education.*

Farnham-Diggory, S. (1994). Paradigms of knowledge and instruction. *Review of Educational Research, 64*(3), 463–477.

Flavell, J. H., & Wellman, H. M. (1977). Metamemory. In R. V. Kail, Jr. & J. W. Hagen (Eds.), *Perspectives and the Development of Memory and Cognition.* Hillsdale, NJ: Erlbaum.

Florida Department of Education. (1990). *Teachers-as-advisors program.* Tallahassee, FL: Division of Public Schools, Bureau of Support Services.

Florida Department of Education. (1991). *Teachers-as-advisors program.* Tallahassee, FL: Division of Public Schools, Bureau of Support Services.

Flowers, N., Mertens, S. B., & Mulhall, P. F. (2000). How teaming influences classroom practices. *Middle School Journal, 32*(2), 52–59.

Foster, W. (1984). Toward a critical theory of educational administration. In T. J. Sergiovanni & J. E. Corbally (Eds.), *Leadership and Organizational Culture.* Urbana, IL: University of Illinois Press.

Fox, R. S. et al. (1974). *School climate improvement: A challenge to the school administration.* Bloomington, IN: Phi Delta Kappa.

Francis W. Parker School Website. (2001). *Francis W. Parker Charter Essential School.* (www.parker.org/curriculum/curriculum.htm).

Frase, L., & Hetzel, R. (1990). *School management by wandering around.* Lancaster, PA: Technomic.

Fullan, M. G. (1993). Coordinating school and district development in restructuring, 143–146. In J. Murphy & P. Hallinger, *Restructuring schools.* Thousands Oaks, CA: Corwin.

Galttorn, A. A. (n.d.). *Learning in the small group.* Abington, PA. (Mimeograph Paper).

Geertz, C. (1973). *The interpretation of culture.* New York: Basic Books.

George, P. S., & Alexander, W. M. (1993). *The exemplary middle school* (2nd ed.). Fort Worth, TX: Harcourt Brace.

Georgiades, W. D. (1978). *How good is your school? Program evaluation for secondary schools.* Reston, VA: National Association of Secondary School Principals.

Georgiades, W. (1991). "School Management Teams," chapter 19. In Keefer, J. W., & Jenkins, J. M. *Instructional leadership handbook* (2nd. ed.). Reston, VA: National Association of Secondary School Principals, 45–46.

Georgiades, W. D., Keefe, J. W., Lowery, R. E., Anderson, W. R., McLean, A. F., Milliken, R., Udinsky, B. F., Warner, W. (1979). *Take five: A methodology for the humane school.* Los Angeles: Parker & Son.

Getzels, J., Lipham, J., & Campbell, R. (1968). *Educational administration as a social process.* New York: Harper & Row.

Glasser, W. (1990). *The quality school: Managing students without coercion.* New York: HarperPerennial.

Glatthorn, A. A. (1995). *Content of the curriculum* (2nd ed.). Alexandria, VA: Association for Supervision and Curriculum Development.

Goldman, J. J. (1983). Flexible modular scheduling: Results of evaluations in its second decade. *Urban Education, 18,* 191–228.

Goodlad, J. I. (1975). *The dynamics of educational change: Toward responsive schools.* New York: McGraw-Hill.

Goodlad, J. L. (1984). *A place called school.* New York: McGraw-Hill.

Gorman, B. W. (1971). *Secondary education: The high school America needs.* New York: Random House.

Gresso, D. (1986). Genesis of the Danforth Preparation Program for School Principals. In M. Milstein (Eds.), *Changing the way we prepare education leaders: The Danforth experience.* Newbury Park, CA: Corwin.

Hackmann, D. G. (1995). Ten guidelines for implementing block scheduling. *Educational Leadership, 53*(3), 28–32.

Hackmann, D. G. (2002). Block scheduling for the middle level: A cautionary tale about the best features of secondary school models. *Middle School Journal, 33*(4), 22–28.

Hackmann, D. G., & Schmitt, D. M. (1997). Strategies for teaching in a block-of-time schedule. *NASSP Bulletin, 81*(588), 1–9.

Hackmann, D. G., & Valentine, J. W. (1998). Designing an effective middle level schedule. *Middle School Journal, 29*(5), 3–13.

Hackmann, D. G., & Waters, D. L. (1998). Breaking away from tradition: The Farmington High School restructuring experience. *NASSP Bulletin, 82*(596), 83–92.

Hallinger, P., & Heck, R. (1996). Reassessing the principal's role in school effectiveness: A review of empirical research. *Educational Administration Quarterly, 32*(1), 5–44.

Hallinger, P., & Murphy, J. F. (1987). Assessing and developing principal instructional leadership. *Educational Leadership, 45*(1), 54–61.

Halpin, A. W. (Ed.). (1958). *Administrative theory in education*. New York: Macmillan.

Halpin, A. W., & Croft, D. (1962). *The organizational climate of schools*. St. Louis, MO: Washington University.

Hersey, P. (n.d.). *NASSP assessment handbook*. Reston, VA: National Association of Secondary School Principals.

Holm, L., & Horn, C. (2003). Bridging the gap between schools of education and the needs of 21st century teachers. *Phi Delta Kappan, 84*(5), 376–380.

House, E. R. (1981). Three perspectives on innovation. In R. Lehman & M. Kane (Eds.), *Improving schools: Using what we know*. Beverly Hills, CA: Sage.

Howard, E. R., Howell, B., & Brainard, E. (1987). *Handbook for conducting school climate improvement projects*. Bloomington, IN: Phi Delta Kappa.

Howard, E. R., & Keefe, J. W. (1991). *The CASE-IMS school improvement process*. Reston, VA: National Association of Secondary School Principals.

Howell, B., & Grahlman, B. (Eds.). (1978). *School climate: Evaluation and implementation*. Tulsa, OK: CADRE.

Hoy, A. W., & Hoy, W. K. (2003). *Instructional leadership: A learning-centered guide*. Boston: Allyn & Bacon.

Hoy, W., & Miskel, C. G. (1987). *Educational administration* (3rd ed.). New York: Random House.

Hughes, L. W., & Ubben, G. C. (1984). *The elementary principal's handbook: A guide to effective action* (2nd ed.). Boston: Allyn & Bacon.

IDEA Website. (2002). *The 35 outcomes of individually guided education.* (www.idea.org/ige35outcomes.htm)

Jackson, A. W., & Davis, G. A. (2000). *Turning points 2000: Educating adolescents in the 21st century.* New York: Teachers College Press.

James, L. R., & McIntyre, M. D. (1996). Perceptions of organizational climate. In K. R. Murphy (Ed.), *Individual differences and behavior in organizations* (pp. 415–450). San Francisco: Jossey-Bass.

Jencks, C. (1972). *Inequality—A reassessment of the effect of family and schooling in America*. New York: Basic Books.

Jenkins, J., & Daniel, B. (2000). *Banishing anonymity: Middle and high school advisement programs*. Larchmont, NY: Eye on Education.

Joyce, B., & Showers, B. (1982). The coaching of teaching. *Educational Leadership*, *40*(1), 4–10.

Keefe, J. W. (1983). Advisement—A helping role. *The Practitioner*, *9*(4). National Association of Secondary School Principals.

Keefe, J. W. (1989). Personalized education. In H. J. Walberg & J. J. Lane (Eds.), *Organizing for learning: Toward the 21st century*. Reston, VA: National Association of Secondary School Principals.

Keefe, J. W., Clark, D. C., Nickerson, N. C., Jr., & Valentine, J. (1983). *The middle level principalship, Volume II: The effective middle level principal*. Reston, VA: National Association of Secondary School Principals.

Keefe, J. W., & Howard, E. R. (1997). *Redesigning schools for the new century: A systems approach*. Reston, VA: National Association of Secondary School Principals.

Keefe, J. W., & Jenkins, J. M. (Eds.). (1991). *Instructional leadership handbook* (2nd ed.). Reston, VA: National Association of Secondary School Principals.

Keefe, J. W., & Jenkins, J. M. (2000). *Personalized instruction: Changing classroom practice*. Larchmont, NY: Eye on Education.

Keefe, J. W., Jenkins, J. M., & Hersey, P. W. (1992). *A leader's guide to school restructuring*. A Special Report of the NASSP Commission on Restructuring. Reston, VA: National Association of Secondary School Principals.

Kennedy, J. F. (1962, September). Address on the nation's space efforts at Rice University. Houston, TX. (John F. Kennedy Library website, www.cs.umb.edu/jfklibrary/j091262.htm)

Kilman, R., Saxton, M., & Serpa, R. (Eds.). (1985). *Gaining control of the corporate culture*. San Francisco: Jossey-Bass.

Kimbrough, R. B., & Burkett, C. W. (1990). *The principalship: Concepts and practices*. Englewood Cliffs, NJ: Prentice-Hall.

Kohn, A. (1999). *The schools our children deserve: Moving beyond traditional classrooms and "tougher standards."* Boston: Houghton Mifflin.

Kosanovic, G. E. (1994). *Retooling the instructional day: A collection of scheduling models*. Reston, VA: National Association of Secondary School Principals.

Kozol, J. (1991). *Savage inequalities: Children in America's schools*. New York: Crown.

Labbe, T. (2002, November 12). Teacher's aides fret over qualification rule. *Washington Post*.

Landers, T. J., & Myers, J. G. (1977). *Essentials of school management.* Philadelphia: W. B. Saunders.

Leithwood, K. A., & Montgomery, D. J. (1982, Fall). The role of the elementary school principal in program improvement. *Review of Educational Research, 52*, 309–339.

Lezotte, L. W. (1990). *Case studies in effective schools research.* The National Center for Effective Schools. Dubuque, IA: Kendall-Hunt.

Lipham, J. M. (1981). *Effective principal, effective schools.* Reston, VA: National Association of Secondary School Principals.

Liu, C. J. (1984). *An identification of principals' instructional leadership in effective high schools.* Unpublished doctoral dissertation, University of Cincinnati.

Lowery, R. E. (1996). Resource centers: A model for academic success. *The High School Magazine, 3*(4) 27–31. Reston, VA: National Association of Secondary School Principals.

Martin, M., & Howard, E. (1998). *The SCA school culture and culture profile.* University of Colorado School of Education.

McCall, J. (1994). *The principal's edge.* Princeton, NJ: Eye on Education.

McChesney, J., & Hertling, E. (2000, April). The path to comprehensive school reform. *Educational Leadership, 57*(7) 10–15.

McCleary, L. E., & Thomson, S. D. (1979). *The senior high school principalship, Volume Three: The summary report.* Reston, VA: National Association of Secondary School Principals.

McCullough, D. (2001). *John Adams.* New York: Simon and Schuster.

McEwan, E. K. (2003). *Seven steps to effective instructional leadership* (2nd ed.). Thousand Oaks, CA: Corwin.

McNeil, J. D. (1996). *Curriculum: A comprehensive introduction* (5th ed.). New York: HarperCollins.

Meier, D. (1995). *The power of their ideas.* Boston: Beacon Press.

Meier, D. (2002, November). Standardization versus standards. *Phi Delta Kappan, 84*(3), 190–198.

Moos, R. (1979). *Evaluating education environments.* San Francisco: Jossey-Bass.

Murphy, J. (1992). *The landscape of leadership preparation: Reframing the education of school administrators.* Newbury Park, CA: Corwin.

National Association of Secondary School Principals. (1969). *The rationale of the NASSP Model Schools Project: Schools of tomorrow.* Study Guide Number 1. Unpublished manuscript. NASSP, Reston, Virginia.

National Association of Secondary School Principals. (1977). Model Schools Project Report. *NASSP Bulletin, 61*(412), 1–142.

National Association of Secondary School Principals. (1996). *Breaking ranks: Changing an American institution*. Reston, VA: National Association of Secondary School Principals.

National Commission for the Principalship. (1990). *Principals for our changing schools: Preparation and certification*. Fairfax, VA: National Commission for the Principalship.

National Commission on Excellence in Education. (1984). *A nation at risk*. Cambridge, MA: USA Research.

National Education Commission on Time and Learning. (1994a). *Prisoners of time: Report of the National Educational Commission on Time and Learning*. Washington, DC: U.S. Government Printing Office.

National Education Commission on Time and Learning. (1994b). *Prisoners of time: Research*. Washington, DC: Author.

National Education Commission on Time and Learning. (1994c). *Prisoners of time: Schools and programs making time work for students and teachers*. Washington, DC: Author.

National Middle School Association. (1995). *This we believe: Developmentally responsive middle level schools*. Columbus, OH: Author.

National Policy Board for Educational Administration. (1993). *Principals for our changing schools: Knowledge and skill base*. Fairfax, VA: National Policy Board for Educational Administration.

Naylor, L. L. (1996). *Culture and change*. Westport, CT: Bergin & Garvey.

Nevis, E. C., DiBella, A. J., & Gould, J. M. (1995, Winter). Understanding organizations as learning systems. *Sloan Management Review*.

New American Schools Website. (2002). *Frequently asked questions* and *Design Team portfolio*. (www.newamericanschools.org)

Newmann, F. M., Secada, W. G., & Wehlage, G. G. (1995). *A guide to authentic instruction and assessment: Vision, standards and scoring*. Madison, WI: Wisconsin Center for Educational Research, University of Wisconsin.

Newmann, F. M., & Wehlage, G. G. (1995). *Successful school restructuring*. A Report to the Public and Educators by the Center on Organization and Restructuring of Schools. Madison, WI: Wisconsin Center for Educational Research, University of Wisconsin.

O'Boyle, T. (1998). *At any cost. Jack Welch, General Electric, and the pursuit of profit*. New York: Vintage Books.

O'Brien, G. P. (1974). *Teacher role change in the NASSP Model Schools Project: A replication*. University of Southern California, Los Angeles. Unpublished doctoral dissertation.

Ornstein, A. C., & Hunkins, F. P. (1998). *Curriculum foundations, principles, and issues* (3rd ed.). Needham Heights, MA: Allyn & Bacon.

Ott, J. S. (1989). *The organizational culture perspective*. Pacific Grove, CA: Brooks/Cole.

Owens, R. G. (2003). *Organizational behavior in education* (8th ed.). Boston: Allyn & Bacon.

Pellicer, L. O., Anderson, L. W., Keefe, J. W., Kelley, E. A., & McCleary, L. E. (1988, 1990). *High school leaders and their schools, Volume I: A national profile. Volume II; Profiles of effectiveness*. Reston, VA: National Association of Secondary School Principals.

Perkins, D. (1992). *Smart schools: Better thinking and learning for every child*. New York: The Free Press.

Powell, A. G., Farrar, E., & Cohen, D. K. (1985). *The shopping mall high school*. Boston: Houghton Mifflin.

Purkey, S. C., & Smith, M. S. (1982, December). Too soon to cheer? Synthesis of research on effective schools. *Educational Leadership*.

Rapp, D. (2002). National board certified teachers in Ohio give state education policy, classroom climate, and high-stakes testing a grade of F. *Phi Delta Kappan, 84*(3), 215–218.

Reilly, D. H. (1984, Spring). The principalship: The need for a new approach. *Education*, 104.

Rettig, M. D., & Canady, R. L.(1999). The effects of block scheduling. *The School Administrator, 56*(3), 14-16i, 18-20.

Robinson, G. (1985, February). Effective schools research: Guide to school improvement. *Concerns in education series*. Arlington, VA: Educational Research Service.

Rutter, M. (1979). *Fifteen thousand hours—Secondary schools and their effects on children*. Cambridge, MA: Harvard University Press.

Sarasan, S. (1971). *The culture of schools and the problem of change*. Boston: Allyn & Bacon.

Sashkin, M., & Egermeier, J. (1991). *School change models and processes: A review of research and practice*. Working draft prepared for the U.S. Department of Education's AMERICA 2000 initiative and for a research symposium at the 1992 annual meeting of the American Educational Research Association, Washington, DC.

Schein, E. H. (1985). *Organizational culture and leadership*. San Francisco: Jossey-Bass.

Schein, E. H. (1993, Winter). How can organizations learn faster? The challenge of entering the green room. *Sloan Management Review*.

Scherer, M. (2001, September). How and why standards can improve student achievement. A conversation with Robert J. Marzano. *Educational Leadership*.

Schlechty, P. (1990). *Schools for the 21st century*. San Francisco: Jossey-Bass.

Schneider, B. (1990). The climate for service: An application of the construct. In B. Schneider (Ed.), *Organizational climate and culture*. San Francisco: Jossey-Bass.

Schwartzbeck, T. D. (2002). *Patterns in implementing comprehensive school reform: What the researchers say*. (Network of Researcher brie {???}; a product of a two day meeting on October 25–26, 2001). Washington, DC: National Clearinghouse for Comprehensive School Reform.

Scott, A. J. (1975). *Evaluating the cognitive achievement of LEC students*. Unpublished doctoral dissertation, University of Southern California.

Seletsky, A. (2000). Afterword. In D. Bensman, *Central Park East and its graduates* (pp. 129–138). New York: Teachers College Press.

Senge, P. M. (1990). *The fifth discipline: The art and practice of the learning organization*. New York: Doubleday.

Sergiovanni, T. (1984, February). Leadership and excellence in schooling. *Educational Leadership, 41*(5), 4, 6-13.

Shriberg, A., Shriberg, D., & Lloyd, C. (2002). *Practicing leadership: Principles and applications* (2nd ed.). New York: John Wiley & Sons.

Simon, K. (1999). *Four essential elements of school design*. CES national website (www.essentialschools.org/cs/cespr/view/ces_res/1).

Sizer, T. (1984). *Horace's compromise: The dilemma of the American high school*. Boston: Houghton Mifflin.

Sizer, T. R. (1992). *Horace's school: Redesigning the American high school*. Boston: Houghton Mifflin.

Sizer, T. R. (1996). *Horace's hope: What works for the American high school*. Boston: Houghton Mifflin.

Sizer, T. R. (1999). *Educational Leadership, 57*(1), 24.

Smircich, L. (1983). Organization as shared meanings. In J. Shafritz & J. S. Ott (Eds.), *Classics of organization theory* (3rd ed.). Belmont, CA: Wadsworth.

Smith, W. F., & Andrews, R. L. (1989). *Instructional leadership: How principals make a difference*. Alexandria, VA: Association for Supervision and Curriculum Development.

Stuffelbeam, D. L., Foley, W. J., Gephart, W. J., Guba, E. G., Hammond, R. L., Merriman, H. O., & Provus, M. M. (1971). *Educational evaluation and decision-making*. PDK Study Committee on Evaluation Report. Itasca, IL: F. E. Peacock.

Sweeny, J. (1982, Winter). Principals can provide instructional leadership: It takes commitment. *Education*, 103.

Tanner, D., & Tanner, L. (1990). *History of the school curriculum*. New York: Macmillan.

Tanner, L. (1997). *Dewey's laboratory school: Lessons for today*. New York: Teachers College Press.

Toffler, B. (2003). *Final Accounting: Ambition, greed, and the fall of Arthur Anderson*. New York: Broadway Books.

Trump, J. L. (1966). Secondary education tomorrow: Four imperatives for improvement. *NASSP Bulletin, 50*(309), 87–95.

Trump, J. L. (1969). Changes needed for further improvement of secondary education in the United States. *NASSP Bulletin, 53*(333), 117–133.

Trump, J. L. (1977). *A school for everyone: Design for a middle, junior, or senior high school that combines the old and the new*. Reston, VA: National Association of Secondary School Principals.

Trump, J. L., & Baynham, D. (1961). *Focus on change: Guide to better schools*. Chicago: Rand McNally.

Trump, J. L., & Georgiades, W. (1970). Doing better with what you have: NASSP Model Schools Project. *NASSP Bulletin, 54*(346), 106–133.

Trump, J. L., & Georgiades, W. (1978). *How to change your school*. Reston, VA: National Association of Secondary School Principals.

Trump, J. L., & Miller, D. F. (1968). *Secondary school curriculum improvement*. Boston: Allyn & Bacon.

Trump, J. L., & Miller, D. F. (1979). *Secondary school curriculum and improvement: Meeting challenges of the time* (3rd ed.). Boston: Allyn & Bacon.

Tyack, D., & Cuban, L. (1995). *Tinkering toward Utopia*. Cambridge, MA: Harvard University Press.

Ubben, G. C., Hughes, L. W., & Norris, C. J. (2001). *The principal: Creative leadership for effective schools* (4th ed.). Needham Heights, NJ: Allyn & Bacon.

Udinsky, B. F., Keefe, J. W., & Housden, J. L. (1972). *Teacher role change in the NASSP Model Schools Project*. Unpublished doctoral dissertation. University of Southern California, Los Angeles.

U.S. Department of Education Website. (2002). *The No Child Left Behind Act of 2001*. Executive Summary. (www.ed.gov/offices/OESE/esea/execsumm.html).

Valentine, J. W., Clark, D. C., Hackmann, D. G., & Petzko, V. N. (2002). *A national study of leadership in middle level schools. Volume I: A national study of middle level leaders and school programs*. Reston, VA: National Association of Secondary School Principals.

Wagner, T. (2003). Reinventing America's schools. *Phi Delta Kappan, 84*(9), 665–668.

Wang, M. C., Haertel, G. U., & Walberg, H. J. (1998). Models of reform: A comparative guide. *Educational Leadership, 55*(7), 66–71.

Wanzare, Z., & Da Costa, J. L. (2001, December). Rethinking instructional leadership roles of the school principal: Challenges and prospects. *Journal of Educational Thought, 35*(3), 269–295.

Wheatley, M. J. (1992). *Leadership and the new science.* San Francisco: Berrett-Koehler.

Williamson, R. D. (1998). *Scheduling middle level schools: Tools for improved student achievement.* Reston, VA: National Association of Secondary School Principals.

Wilson, C. (1995). The 4:5 block system: A workable alternative. *NASSP Bulletin, 79*(571), 63–65.

Windschitl, M. (1999). The challenges of sustaining a constructivist classroom culture. *Phi Delta Kappan, 80,* 751–755.

Wolcott, H. (1973). *Man in the principal's office.* New York: Holt, Rinehart, & Winston.

Woods, G. H. (1992). *Schools that work: America's most innovative public education programs.* New York: Penguin Books USA (Plume).

Index

106, 110, 111, 113, 128, 131,
142, 145, 148, 156, 159, 167,
174
curriculum design, 11, 95, 180
Cushman, K., 60, 189

Da Costa, J. L., 176, 199
Dalin, P., 125, 189
Danforth Program for the
Preparation of School Principals,
36
Daniel, B., 134, 193
Dantley, M., 97, 189
Daresh, J. C., 34, 45, 189
Darling-Hammond, L., 59, 124, 157,
177, 189
Davis, G. A., 88, 192
Deal, T. E., 125, 127, 133, 189
defined, 14, 32, 56, 64, 73, 77, 101,
129, 133, 148, 181,
defining school climate, 129
defining school culture, 127
Deming, W. E., 165, 189
Dewey, John, 5, 10, 123, 173
Dewey's progressive education
movement, 173
diagnosis, 12, 15, 111, 112, 142,
143
diagnosis, prescription,
implementation, and evaluation
(DPIE), vii, 12, 15, 111, 112,
142, 143
diagnosis, prescription,
implementation, and evaluation
(DPIE) model, 15, 70, 113
DiBella, A. J., 40, 195
differentiated staffing, 11, 29, 52,
133, 142
differentiated staffing model, 51
Duguid, P., 118, 188

Dykema, R., 21, 189

Edgewood Junior High School in
Mounds, 144
Edmonds, R., 27, 129, 130, 190
Education Commission of the States,
9, 190
Educational Administration as a
Social Process, 34
Educational Research Service, 35,
190
effectiveness of the principal, 34, 48
Egermeier, J., 3, 196
eight-year study, 99, 124, 173
Eisner, E. W., 122, 156, 190
Elmore, R. F., 8, 190
empowerment, 30, 88
English, F. W., 8, 79, 119, 190
ERIC Clearinghouse on Educational
Management, 47, 190
evaluation, 11, 12, 13, 14, 17, 24,
25, 26, 29, 2, 45, 46, 51, 64, 66,
67, 68, 112, 114, 119, 132, 139,
140, 141, 142, 144, 145, 148,
150, 155, 159, 166, 174, 182
external evaluations, 149

Falk, B., 157, 189
Farnham-Diggory, S., 61, 190
Farrar, E., 58, 196
Flavell, J. H., 67, 190
flexible interdisciplinary schedule
with daily periods, 90, 91
flexible modular scheduling, 75
flexible schedules with
interdisciplinary blocks, 81, 86
Florida Department of Education,
60, 190
Flowers, N., 89, 190
Foster, W., 31, 47, 190

About the Editors and Contributors

Jack Frymier was born and raised in Indiana. He received his bachelor's and master's degrees from the University of Miami and his doctorate from the University of Florida. Frymier served in the U.S. Army during World War II and the Korean War. He has been a public school teacher, administrator, university professor, and researcher, and he is currently professor emeritus at The Ohio State University. His major areas of interest are motivation, values, risk factors, human development, program development, and public policy.

Ronald G. Joekel is currently professor emeritus at the University of Nebraska-Lincoln teaching classes via online distance education. He is emeritus executive director of Phi Delta Kappa International, having retired from Phi Delta Kappa in 2000. He has held positions as a high school principal and K–12 school superintendent, and he is a former associate dean of the Teachers College and Chair of the Department of Educational Administration at the University of Nebraska. Activity in professional organizations has earned him 18 distinguished service awards.

Robert B. Amenta is associate professor of education and director of educational administration at California Lutheran University, Thousand Oaks, California.

Cliff (Clifton) Colia is principal of Carbondale Middle School in Colorado. He recently completed his dissertation on *Culture, Climate, and*

School Effectiveness at the University of Colorado and is now actively providing leadership with at-risk youth.

Fenwick W. English is R. Wendell Eaves distinguished professor of educational leadership in the School of Education at the University of North Carolina at Chapel Hill.

Donald G. Hackmann is associate professor and educational administration program coordinator in the Department of Educational Leadership and Policy Studies at Iowa State University.

Eugene R. Howard designed and operated one of the first "Trump Plan" schools. He is a former associate superintendent in San Francisco; former superintendent in Urbana, Illinois; former director for school improvement and leadership, Colorado State Department of Education; and an active member of LEC and the Kettering Foundation.

John M. Jenkins is vice president of Learning Environments Consortium International and former high school principal in the Model School Project.

James W. Keefe is the retired director of research for the National Association of Secondary School Principals, and he is president of Learning Environments Consortium International. His professional experience includes junior high, senior high, and university teaching and secondary school administration.

Robert E. Lowery is founding principal of Bishop Carroll High School in Calgary, Alberta and is superintendent of personal and academic excellence for a Charter School.

Michael Martin is associate vice president, University of Colorado; past president of the National Council of Professors of Educational Administration; and former school administrator in Santa Barbara City and County Schools.